FABULOUS MONSTERS

Alberto Manguel

Fabulous
Monsters

Dracula, Alice, Superman, and Other
Literary Friends

With Illustrations by the Author

Yale UNIVERSITY PRESS   NEW HAVEN & LONDON

Published with support from the Fund established in memory of Oliver
Baty Cunningham, a distinguished graduate of the Class of 1917, Yale
College, Captain, 15th United States Field Artillery, born in Chicago
September 17, 1894, and killed while on active duty near Thiaucourt,
France, September 17, 1918, the twenty-fourth anniversary of his birth.

Yale University Press books may be purchased in quantity for
educational, business, or promotional use. For information, please e-mail
sales.press@yale.edu (U.S. office) or sales@yaleup.co.uk (U.K. office).

Designed by Nancy Ovedovitz. Set in Bembo and
Scala Sans Bold types by Integrated Publishing Solutions.
Printed in the United States of America.

Library of Congress Control Number: 2019936416
ISBN 978-0-300-24738-1 (hardcover : alk. paper)

A catalogue record for this book is available from the British Library.

This paper meets the requirements of ANSI/NISO Z39.48–1992
(Permanence of Paper).

10 9 8 7 6 5 4 3 2 1

To Amelia, who
likes princesses, and
to Olivia, who prefers
dragons

AMELIA & OLIVIA

CONTENTS

PREFACE

"This is a child!" Haigha replied eagerly, coming in front of Alice to introduce her, and spreading out both his hands towards her in an Anglo-Saxon attitude. "We only found it to-day. It's as large as life, and twice as natural!"

"I always thought they were fabulous monsters!" said the Unicorn. "Is it alive?"

"It can talk," said Haigha solemnly.

The Unicorn looked dreamily at Alice, and said "Talk, child."

Alice could not help her lips curling up into a smile as she began: "Do you know, I always thought Unicorns were fabulous monsters, too? I never saw one alive before!"

"Well, now that we *have* seen each other," said the Unicorn, "if you'll believe in me, I'll believe in you. Is that a bargain?"

LEWIS CARROLL, *Through the Looking-Glass*

Tourist guides offer excursions along the arduous paths of Odysseus and Don Quixote. Crumbling buildings are said to house Desdemona's bedchamber and Juliet's balcony. A Colombian village assures us that it is the Macondo of Aureliano Buendía, and the island of Juan Fernandez boasts of having welcomed, centuries ago, that singular imperialist Robinson Crusoe. For many years now, the British Postal Service has busied itself with correspondence addressed to Mr. Sherlock Holmes, Esq., at 221B Baker Street, while Charles Dickens used to receive an angry stream of letters blaming him for the death of Little Nell in *The Old Curiosity Shop*. Biology tells us that we descend from creatures of flesh and blood, but intimately we know that we are the sons and daughters of ghosts of ink and paper. Ages ago, Luis de Góngora defined them with these words:

> In his playhouse built on lofty drapes,
> Sleep, the author of dramatic scenes,
> Dresses up phantoms of becoming shapes.

The term *fiction* entered the English language in the early fifteenth century with the meaning "something invented or imagined." It derived, etymological dictionaries tell us, via the French, from the past participle of the Latin verb *fingere,* which originally meant "to knead or form out of clay." Fiction is then a sort of verbal Adam molded from the primordial dust in the Author's image and infused by the Author with the breath of life. Perhaps that is why, contrary to appearances, fictional characters at their best often seem more alive than our friends of solid flesh. Far from sticking to their stories, they change the plot at every one of our readings, bringing certain scenes to light and obscuring others, adding a startling episode that we had mysteriously forgotten or a detail that previously remained unnoticed. Heraclitus's warning about time is true for every reader: we never step twice into the same book.

For readers, the revelation of the world frequently occurs in the pages of their books. When Alice, in *Through the Looking-Glass,* meets Humpty Dumpty perched precariously on a narrow wall, she solicitously asks him if he doesn't think he'd be safer down on the ground. "Of course I don't think so!" Humpty growls back. "Why, if ever I *did* fall off—which there's no chance of—but *if* I did—" he makes a solemn pause, "*The King has promised me—with his very own mouth—to—to* . . ." "To send all his horses and all his men," Alice interrupts, rather unwisely. Humpty breaks into a sudden passion. "You've been listening at doors—and behind trees—and down chimneys—or you couldn't have known it!" he cries. "I haven't, indeed!" Alice answers very gently. "It's in a book." No true reader would find Alice's explanation surprising.

Readers around the world express veneration for the likes of Shakespeare and Cervantes, but these beings, immortalized in hopeful and stern portraits, are less tangible than their immortal creations. King Lear and Lady Macbeth, Don Quixote and Dulcinea are real presences even for many of those who have never read their books. We are acquainted with the entangled passions of Queen Dido and of Don Juan far more than with the intimate lives of Virgil and Molière, except in those aspects revealed in the novels of Hermann Broch and Mikhail Bulgakov. Readers have always known that the dreams of fiction give birth to the world we call real.

Dante was well aware of this. In Canto IV of the *Inferno,* after passing through the terrible gates that banish all hope, Virgil shows Dante the Noble Castle that houses the souls of the just who were born before the coming of Christ. Among the men and women of sorrowful slow eyes whom Dante sees there, he notices Aeneas, the hero dreamt up by Virgil, and mentions him with just two words: "ed Enea." Dante seems to understand that if he must grant Virgil the complex reality required as one of the three main protagonists of his *Commedia,* the imaginary character (Aeneas) cannot have the same literary weight as the character who imagined him (Virgil). Aeneas exists in the *Commedia,* but only as a fleeting shadow, so that Virgil can become rooted in the reader's mind not just as the historical author of the *Aeneid* but as the memorable traveling companion in Dante's road trip.

In my adolescence, thanks to a quirky high school teacher, we read a few of the writings of Edmund Husserl on phenomenology, which, to our idealistic minds, sounded enthralling. While most of the adult world seemed to insist that only tangible things were worth caring for, Husserl, to our delight, argued that we can forge a bond, even a deep bond, with things that are deemed inexistent. Mermaids and unicorns, as far as we know, have no proven tangible existence, even though medieval Chinese bestiaries declare that the reason unicorns are not often seen is because of their extreme natural shyness. And yet, Husserl argued, the human mind can be intentionally directed towards those imaginary beings and create between us and them what he unpoetically calls "a normal dyadic relationship." I have established many such relationships with hundreds of these creatures.

But not every literary character is the chosen companion of every reader; only those we love best follow us throughout our years. As far as I'm concerned, I don't feel as mine the doubtless heart-wrenching troubles of Renzo and Lucia in *I promessi sposi,* of Mathilde de la Mole and Julien Sorel in *Le Rouge et le noir,* of the status-conscious Bennet family in *Pride and Prejudice.* I'm closer to the vengeful wrath of the Count of Monte Cristo, to the stalwart self-confidence of Jane Eyre, to the reasoned melancholy of Valéry's Monsieur Teste. My more intimate comrades are many: Chesterton's Man Who Was Thursday magically helps me cope with the absurdities of everyday life; Priam teaches me to weep for the death of younger friends, and Achilles for that of my beloved elders; Little Red Riding Hood and Dante the Pilgrim guide me through the dark forests of the road of life; Sancho's neighbor, the exiled Ricote, allows me to understand something of the infamous notion of prejudice. And there are so many more!

Perhaps one of the main attractions of these fabulous monsters is their multiple and changing identities. Rooted in their own histories, fictional characters cannot be caged between the covers of their books, however brief or vast that space might be. Hamlet is born already grown into adulthood under the blind arcades of Elsinore, and dies still young among a pile of corpses in one of the castle's feasting halls, but generations of readers have rescued from the unscripted darkness both his Freudian childhood and his posthumous political career—for instance in the Third Reich, where he became the most performed character on the German stage. Tom Thumb has increased in size, Helen has become a wizened hag, Balzac's Rastignac works for the International Monetary Fund, Odysseus has been shipwrecked on the coast of Lampedusa, Kim has been recruited into the British Ministry of Foreign Affairs, Pinocchio is languishing in a concentration camp for children in Texas, the Princesse de Clèves has been forced to seek employment on Skid Row. Unlike their readers, who grow old and never become young again, fictional characters are, at the same time, those who they were when we read their stories for the first time, and those who they have become in our successive readings. Every fictional character is like Proteus, the sea god to whom Poseidon granted the power of transforming himself into any of the shapes in the universe. "I know who I am," Don Quixote says in one of his earliest adventures, after a neighbor tries to convince him that he is not one of the imaginary persons in the knight's beloved novels of chivalry. "And I know that I can be not only those I've mentioned, but all the Twelve Peers of France, and even the Nine Worthies, because my achievements will excel, not only each of them singly, but even the deeds of all of them together." Don Quixote empathetically assumes the myriad identities of the characters in his books.

More etymologies. Like *sympathy*, *empathy* derives from the Greek root *pathos* meaning "to endure or to undergo." The word *empathes* with the sense of "much affected by" appears seldom in the Greek corpus. Aristotle, for example, employs the term only once in the sixth book of his treatise *On Dreams,* to refer to the intense fear experienced by a coward who dreams that his enemies are approaching. In English, *empathy* is a fairly recent invention. It was coined in 1909 by a psychologist at Cornell University, Edward Bradford Titchner, who suggested the term as a translation of the German *Einfühlung.* According to Titchner, this emotional impulse to "feel into" something or someone is a strategy that we employ to find in external examples (as in Aristotle's coward's dreams) solutions for our mental conflicts. Empathy, Titchner suggests, heals the self.

David Hume arrived there earlier. In 1738, in his *Treatise on Human Nature,* he observed that "'Tis indeed evident, that when we sympathize with the passions and sentiments of others, these movements appear at first in our mind as mere ideas, and are conceiv'd to belong to another person, as we conceive any other matter of fact. 'Tis also evident, that the ideas of the affections of others are converted into the very impressions they represent, and that the passions arise in conformity to the images we form of them." Husserl would say that those "others" need not be of flesh and blood.

My own experience has been Husserlian. One can build one's autobiography in many ways: through the places one has lived, through the dreams one has had and still remembers, through remarkable encounters with unfading men and women, through mere chronological accounting. I have always thought of my life as the turning of the pages of many books. My readings, the ones that form my imaginary cartography, define almost every one of my intimate experiences, and I can trace back to a certain paragraph or line most everything I believe I know about the essential things.

Those pages of far away and long ago include the experiences of today. In our own anguished times, the forced migrations, the persistently hopeful refugees, the shipwrecked asylum seekers washed up on the European coast are all reflected in the figure of Odysseus trying to find his home. In a study conducted in 1992 by a researcher at the University of Guadalajara in Mexico, one of the migrant workers interviewed described his experience of trying to reach the United States: "The north is like the sea," the man said. "When one travels as an illegal, one is dragged like the tail of an animal, like trash. I imagined how the sea washes trash onto the shore, and I told myself, maybe it's just like I'm in the ocean, being tossed out again and again." This is Odysseus's experience after leaving Calypso in a renewed attempt to reach Ithaca, yet fearing he'll come to a pitiable end. "As he spoke, a wave broke over him with such terrific fury that the raft reeled again, and he was carried overboard a long way off. He let go the helm, and the force of the storm was so great that it broke the mast, and both sail and spar fell into the sea. For a long time Odysseus was under the water, struggling to rise to the surface again, because the clothes Calypso had given him weighed him down. But finally he got his head above the waves and spat out the brine that was running down his face. He did not, however, lose sight of the raft, but swam as fast as he could towards it and climbed on board again. But the sea took the raft and tossed it about as autumn winds toss thistledown round and round on dry land."

The experience of the world—love, death, friendship, loss, gratitude, bewilderment, anguish, fear—all these and my own changing identity, I have learned from the imaginary characters I've met throughout my readings, much more than through my shadowy face in the mirror or my reflection in the eyes of others. Eliot has these lines in *The Waste Land:*

> And I will show you something different from
>   either
> Your shadow at morning striding behind you
> Or your shadow at evening rising to meet you;
> I will show you fear in a handful of dust.

My feelings exactly.

The earliest "handful of dust" to show me fear that I can remember was the handsome Robber Bridegroom in the Grimms' fairy tale, whose promised bride arrives secretly at his house to discover that he is the leader of a band of murderers. Hiding behind a barrel, she sees her future bridegroom and his mates drag into the house a screaming, sobbing girl. "They gave her wine to drink, three glasses full, one glass of white, one glass of red, and one glass of yellow, which caused her heart to break. Then they ripped off her fine clothes, laid her on a table, chopped her beautiful body in pieces and sprinkled salt on it." The story ends, of course, with the punishment of the criminals "for their shameful deeds," but that was not the end for me. Robert Louis Stevenson said that he had a recurrent nightmare of "a certain hue of brown, which he did not mind in the least while he was awake, but feared and loathed while he was dreaming." I was haunted for endless nights by the three colors of the wine reflecting their prism light on the bits of dismembered body.

Because my father was a diplomat, my childhood was largely spent traveling from place to place. The bedrooms in which I slept, the words spoken outside the door, the landscapes around me constantly changed. Only my small library remained the same, and I remember the intense relief I felt when, tucked once again in an unfamiliar bed, I opened my books and there on the expected page was the same old story and the same old illustration. Home was a place in stories, both in the physical object I held in my hands and in the printed words. When Mole, in *The Wind in the Willows,* returns to his little house from the big outside world, and lets his eyes wander round the old room, and sees how plain and simple it all is, and understands how much it means to him, I remember feeling something like pangs of envy, knowing that he had somewhere to come back to, a "place which was all his own, these things which were so glad to see him again and could always be counted upon for the same simple welcome."

Love came to me at about the time I turned eight and we returned to Buenos Aires, and I was given a room of my own in which I could keep my books. It came at more or less the same moment as fear had come, and also through one of the Grimms' fairy tales, "The True Sweetheart," a subtler version of the Cinderella story in which the lovers know from the start that they are meant for each other, and after a few magical obstacles live happily ever after. I knew that somewhere my as yet faceless sweetheart was certainly waiting for me. Later on, in my adolescence, when I began to feel the first erotic stirrings, I was terrified that if I declared my feelings then and there, my explicitness would be seen as offensive and off-putting. Juliet's words to Romeo warned me against artificial coyness: "If thou think'st I am too quickly won, I'll frown and be perverse and say thee nay, so thou wilt woo; but else, not for the world." I followed her advice with mixed results.

When finally I fell truly in love for the first time and tried to understand my mixed emotions of bewilderment, contentment, and triumph, the line with which Kipling's *Kim* ends, about how the Lama felt about his *chela,* made it clear to me: "He crossed his hands on his lap and smiled, as a man may who has won salvation for himself and his beloved." I also found an echo of my blind head-over-heels devotion in the words the beheaded disciple Ling speaks to his master in Marguerite Yourcenar's oriental tale "How Wang Fo Was Saved." Wang Fo, seeing the ghost of his disciple appear before him, says to him: "I thought you were dead." And Ling answers, "With you alive, how could I die?" How indeed?

Sadegh Hedayat assures us in *The Blind Owl* that "throughout our lives, the finger of death points at us." Thanks to *The Blind Owl* and other stories, I feel now that I have at least a pocket guide to that finger-pointing presence to help me once I reach it. To begin with, I know it will be a verb, not a noun. When the narrator in André Malraux's *La voie royale* mentions death to his agonizing friend, the man reacts with indignant anger:

"There is . . . no death . . . There's only . . . me . . . me . . . who's dying." And Tolstoy's Ivan Ilych describes for me what that feeling of coming to an end might resemble: "What had happened to him was like the sensation one sometimes experiences in a railway carriage when one thinks one is going backwards while one is really going forwards and suddenly becomes aware of the real direction." I believe I know exactly what he means. However, if I could choose my death, I'd choose that of the writer Bergotte in Proust's saga: "All through that night of mourning, in the lighted windows, his books, arranged three by three, kept vigil like angels with outspread wings and seemed, for him who was no more, the symbol of his resurrection."

In moments of indecision, in moments of anguish, in moments of doubt, the Scarecrow's advice to Dorothy upon coming to the Dark Wood is always helpful to me because of its basic common sense: "If this road goes in, it must come out," he says, "and as the Emerald City is at the other end of the road, we must go wherever it leads us." Indeed. And when our traveling companions are not as encouraging as the Scarecrow, I think of the old father in Juan Rulfo's story "Can't You Hear the Dogs Bark?" carrying his wounded son Ignacio on his back to get him to the doctor in the distant village. Ignacio does not understand that he should give his exhausted father encouragement by telling him that he hears the village dogs bark, even though he doesn't. "And you didn't hear them, Ignacio?" the father says to him at the end, when they finally arrive. "You didn't even help me listen."

Friendship, partnership, loving care entail helping to

listen for what is not yet there, might never be there. Virginia Woolf portrays the frustration of this hope at beginning of *To the Lighthouse,* when Mrs. Ramsay promises her six-year-old son James an excursion to the lighthouse "if it's fine tomorrow." "But," his father says, stopping in front of the drawing-room window, "it won't be fine." And Woolf comments, "Had there been an axe handy, a poker, or any weapon that would have gashed a hole in his father's breast and killed him, there and then, James would have seized it." I often feel the same vengeful impulse as James's and want to take revenge on the objective, paternalistic world, and like King Lear "do such things—what they are, yet I know not: but they shall be the terrors of the earth."

Not only in love, death, and revenge do my imaginary friends assist and counsel me. In my writing too, they occasionally provide help. The best piece of advice for getting down to work when inspiration fails was given to me by Harriet Vane, the detective-story writer in Dorothy L. Sayers's *Gaudy Night.* Lord Peter Wimsey, the aristocratic sleuth, has saved her from the gallows in a previous novel and wants to marry her, but how can she enter a balanced relationship with someone to whom she owes her life? In *Gaudy Night,* Harriet is trying to compose a letter to Wimsey about a delicate matter concerning his nephew but she cannot find the right tone. After trying and failing again and again, she finally says to herself: "What is the matter with me? Why can't I write a straightforward piece of English on a set subject?" And then she sits down and does it. More times than I can say, this stern admonition has helped me get my job done.

Occasionally, the advice is excellent, but I find myself incapable of following it, as when the King in *Alice in Wonderland* says to the White Rabbit: "Begin at the beginning, and go on till you come to the end: then stop." Or when Jo in *Little Women* shuts herself up in her room, puts on her "scribbling suit," and "falls into a vortex," as she calls it, writing away with all her heart and soul, "for till that was finished she could find no peace." I can seldom drum up such persistent creative energy.

What has become a cornerstone of faith for me, truer than true, and more so as time goes by, are the words the Abbot says to the painter of illuminations, in Kipling's story "The Eye of Allah": "But for the pain of the soul there is, outside God's Grace, but one drug; and that is a man's craft, learning, or other helpful motions of his own mind." My imaginary friends assist me to achieve such helpful motions.

In that most compelling of autobiographies *Father and Son,* Edmund Gosse explains that works of fiction were not admitted into his parents' stern Calvinist household. "Never in all my early childhood, did anyone address to me the affecting preamble, 'Once upon a time!' I was told about missionaries, but never about pirates; I was familiar with humming-birds, but I had never heard of fairies. Jack the Giant-Killer, Rumpelstiltskin and Robin Hood were not of my acquaintance, and though I understood about wolves, Little Red Ridinghood was a stranger even by name. So far as my 'dedication' was concerned, I can but think that my parents were in error thus to exclude the imaginary from my outlook upon facts. They desired to make me truthful; the tendency was to make me positive and sceptical. Had they wrapped me in the soft folds of supernatural fancy, my mind might have been longer content to follow their traditions in an unquestioning spirit."

In the distant childhood of my generation, wrapped in the soft folds of supernatural fancy, our playmates were Pippi Longstocking and Pinocchio, Sandokan the Pirate and Mandrake the Magician; those of today's children are presumably Harry Potter and his companions, and Maurice Sendak's Wild Things. All these fabulous monsters are so unconditionally faithful that they are untroubled by our weaknesses and failures. Now that my bones barely allow me to reach the lowest shelves, Sandokan calls me once more to arms, and Mandrake compels me to seek vengeance against fools, while Pippi, with great patience, tells me again and again not to give a hoot about conventions and to follow my own nose, and Pinocchio keeps on asking me why, in spite of what the Blue Fairy has told him, it isn't enough to be honest and good in order to be happy. And I, as in the days far away and long ago, cannot find the right answer.

FABULOUS MONSTERS

MONSIEUR BOVARY

Of the two, he is the second fiddle, the more prosaic, the least impulsive, the one resigned to a decent state of anonymity, the one with whom Flaubert does not identify. He is the one who gives Emma an excuse for her infidelity, though he has never demanded that she be faithful to him. He is the one who leads an honest, regular, hard-working life, with no other ambition than that of quiet contentment, with no surprises. True, he lacks charm. No one feels for him an all-consuming

passion, no one imagines him climbing balconies at night or fighting a duel in a snow-covered glade. And yet, Monsieur Bovary is an absolutely necessary character. Let us remember that *Madame Bovary* begins and ends with him, not with Emma. Without him, Emma would have no meaning, she would never become a romantic heroine, she would never know passion or ecstatic bliss. Let me be clear: Monsieur Bovary exists so that Madame can fulfill her tragic destiny.

The truth is that Charles Bovary lacks imagination. His rather stolid behavior is the fruit of a lackluster life drawn in black and white. Even as a boy, he is a bit of a nerd. In the first pages of the novel, Flaubert describes him as a clumsy and timorous adolescent who can barely say his name in answer to the teacher's question. He inspires neither trust nor tenderness. On the first day of class, the teacher has him copy out twenty times "I'm ridiculous." The boy makes no complaint. Later, it is his father who decides that he will study medicine and his mother who chooses for him a place to live. Charles, who has now become Monsieur Bovary, allows others to make all decisions for him.

Artistic truth is alien to his spirit. Sentimental fiction ("women's novels" as he calls them), in which Emma finds her models, has no meaning him. For Monsieur Bovary, fiction does not exist. In the theater, attending with Emma a performance of *Lucia di Lammermoor* and seeing the passion with which Edgar declares his love for the heroine, he wonders, "But this gentleman, why is he harassing her?" "But no," Emma answers impatiently. "He's her lover." Charles still does not understand. "Oh shut up!" Emma snaps back. Innocently, he defends himself: "It's just that, as you know, I like to understand what's going on." Emma cannot make him see that, just as when one attends an opera, amorous passion in real life cannot be explained: one has a gut understanding of the thing, or one is excluded from it forever. In matters such as these, Monsieur Bovary is for the most part the outsider.

Lucia's tragic story and Donizetti's music make Emma recall her wedding day. Compared to the ecstatic passion lived out onstage by the performers, the joy of those long-past hours seems to her "a lie imagined because there was no hope for desire." This is a curious observation: Emma conceives artistic creation as something that stems not from our desires but from our lack of desire. What does this tell us about Flaubert himself, who spent his life fulfilling (or attempting to fulfill) his erotic fantasies? If he believed in what he has Emma believe, what should we believe, we, his readers? His own desires or his art? After all, "Madame Bovary c'est moi!" is Flaubert's best-known line.

Literary spouses are not all self-effacing. Andromache, Clytemnestra, Lady Macbeth have their roles to play, as or more vigorous and memorable as those of their marriage partners. True, Acerbas (husband of Dido), Donna Ximena (wife of El Cid), Alexei Alexandrovich Karenin (husband of Anna) are somewhat vaguer, but few I think have the simultaneously discreet and necessary counterbalancing effect of Charles Bovary.

Passion, imaginative talent, originality, charm—all might be lacking in Monsieur Bovary, but not love. Monsieur Bovary loves his wife. After her death, he strives hard not to forget her, and yet day after day her beloved image seems gradually to fade, and poor Monsieur Bovary is left inconsolable. Only in his dreams does he manage to bring her back as she was: every night he sees her, and he goes towards her, but when he tries to embrace her, Emma dissolves in a mass of rotting flesh.

Shortly after Emma's death, as an example of literary even-handedness, Monsieur Bovary dies sitting on the same garden bench on which Emma had conducted her amorous affair. Before dying, he forgives his wife's lover, assures him that he bears him no ill, and says out loud: "Only destiny is to blame!" These are his final words. Maliciously, as a kind of posthumous insult, Flaubert lends the poor man a cliché that would have delighted those future clowns Bouvard and Pécuchet.

But therein lies a paradox. That romantic and trivial literature that Flaubert so obviously despises, and that so greatly delights Emma and no doubt contributes to her misfortune, lends Monsieur Bovary a fitting epitaph. The words on Emma's tomb are "amabilem conjugem calcas!": "You are treading on a beloved wife!"—which is neither sentimental nor funny, merely grotesque. However, saying that destiny is ultimately guilty of the kind of life we have led, whether tragic or happy, even if doubtless a cliché, is not for that reason less a truth: immutable, literary, and—why not say so?—brave.

LITTLE RED RIDING HOOD

There are characters whose name reveals their skin color (Snow White), their ability (Spiderman), their size (Thumbelina). Others, their dress. A short blood-colored cape defines the adventurous girl dreamt up by Charles Perrault towards the end of the seventeenth century. She has a whiff of the guileless temptress, this creature who is at the same time polite and daring, and who exudes something so subtly attractive that it made the adult Charles Dickens confess that she had been his first love.

"I felt that if I could have married Little Red Riding Hood," he admitted, "I should have known perfect bliss."

Her story is well known: the errand on which her mother sends her (to deliver a cake and a pot of butter to her sick grandmother), the meeting with the treacherous beast (pivotal to the story), the distractions she finds on her way (picking up acorns and pursuing butterflies), the tragic fate of the grandmother (reminiscent of the fate of both Jonah and Gepetto), her questioning of the impersonator and the cross-dressing wolf's answers that end up revealing the true identity of the fiend (a catechism commonplace in folktales).

A precursor of the story is tucked away in the *Prose Edda,* composed in Iceland in the thirteenth century. It tells how Loki, the trickster, must explain to the giant Thrym why the giant's betrothed (who is none other than Thor, the god of thunder, in disguise) has such a decidedly unfeminine aspect.

"I've never seen a bride eat and drink so much," says the bewildered Thrym after watching the supposed lady devour eight salmons and a whole ox.

"That's because she was so anxious to see you," Loki answers, "that she didn't eat anything for eight days."

"Why does she have such a terrible look?" asks Thrym, perceiving the fierce thundering eyes behind the bridal veil.

"That's because she was so anxious to see you," Loki answers once more, "that she hasn't slept in eight long nights."

Our stories are full of travestied characters: female into male is commonplace in Shakespeare—Rosalind,

Portia, Imogen, Viola—as is male into female: Falstaff as Mistress Ford's fat aunt. Huckleberry Finn dressed up as a girl called Sarah or Mary, Mr. Rochester as an old gypsy fortune-teller, Toad in *The Wind in the Willows* as an old washerwoman: all survive by playing the catechism of conventional identity against itself.

Little Red Riding Hood's credo is that of Thoreau: civil disobedience. Her mother's autocratic orders must be followed, this she knows, but she will follow them in her own sweet time. Not for her the shortest path between A and Z, not for her straight and narrow. Holden Caulfield in *The Catcher in the Rye* would have approved. "I *like* it when somebody digresses," he says. "It's more *int*eresting and all." Because of her digressions, the woods come into being, and also the wolf, the woodcutter, the grandmother's romantic adventure. Without Little Red Riding Hood's digressive spirit there would be no story.

Zeno argued that movement was impossible because in order to proceed from any given place to the next, we have to reach a point halfway between the two, and to reach that we have to reach another halfway between the first and the intermediate one, and so on throughout eternity. Little Red Riding Hood proves Zeno wrong. Movement is possible exactly because of all these intermediate points: points in the landscape in which the berries are ripe, the acorns plentiful, the flowers ready to be picked. Even the presence of the wolf is only one more intermediate point on the way to her grandmother's house (which she *will* eventually reach) because this disobedient girl (disobedient of both maternal and pre-Socratic laws) chooses the points at which she will stop of her own free will. Little Red Riding Hood is emblematic of individual freedom, which is perhaps why the hood of France's revolutionary Marianne is the same color as hers.

Little Red Riding Hood's story changes according to who is telling it. In Perrault's tale, she is devoured by the wolf and that is the end. Later versions, more compassionate, bring in a heroic woodcutter, who appears at the last moment to save the child from the wolf's maw and, by means of a sort of caesarean operation, rescue the grandmother as well. Perrault does not describe the scene where Little Red Riding Hood gets into bed with the fake grandmother, but thanks to the moral that concludes the tale it becomes clear what type of wolf Perrault had in mind. "Not all wolves are the same," he writes. "There are those who cunningly, without trumpeting their intentions, neither hot-blooded nor spiteful, very discreetly, complacent and well-behaved, follow young ladies to their homes and even to their beds. But, beware! Who ignores that these sweet-sounding wolves are, of all the wolves, the most dangerous?"

The strategy of the wolf is employed more often than we know. The notorious abbot of Choisy, Perrault's contemporary, behaved in this ungentlemanly manner. Even as a boy (he tells us in his memoirs) he liked dressing up in women's clothing. In Bourges, where he had gone to spend a short cross-dressing holiday, he met a certain Madame Gaillot, whose youngest daughter was a very pretty child. One evening, Madame Gaillot suggested that her daughter sleep in the same bed as her guest. The abbot, in his frilly nightgown and ribboned cap, readily agreed. After a time, the girl shouted out: "Ah me! What pleasure!" "Are you not asleep, my daughter?" the mother called out upon hearing her moan. "It's just that I was cold getting into bed," the clever girl replied. "But now that I'm warm I feel very, very content."

Almost a century after the abbot's escapade, the Marquis de Sade understood that Little Red Riding Hood's story could bear a different reading. "There is no infamy that the wolf does not invent in order to capture his prey," he warned from his cell in the Charenton Asylum for the Insane. If this is true—if almost whatever Little Red Riding Hood does, she is likely to end up in the wolf's bed—she still has two possible strategies for escape. The first is to resign herself to her condition of victimhood (a theme Sade developed in *Justine; or, The Misfortunes of Virtue*), the second to become mistress of her own fate (as he explored in *Juliet; or, The Prosperities of Vice*).

Both these strategies have produced descendants. Daughters of the former are Dumas's Camille, Galdós's Marianela, Dickens's Little Dorrit; of the latter are Shaw's Mrs. Warren, Nabokov's Lolita, and Vargas Llosa's Bad Girl. Little Red Riding Hood, however, is both types at once. Seduced seducer, worldly innocent, she keeps on roaming the woods, free and unafraid of disingenuous wolves.

DRACULA

It seems that sometime in the fifteenth century, a certain Vlad Draculesti, prince of Wallachia, ruled over a fair part of what is now Romania with such ferociousness that his subjects, in reference to the prince's favorite method of torture, gave him the name Vlad the Impaler. In spite of the ambitious number of his victims (more than ten thousand) and his reputed delight in the suffering of others (he would say that the smell of human blood gave him better nourishment than roast duck with

plums), Vlad Draculesti seems not unlike the pack of rulers who were his elders or disciples: Herod and Nero, Pol Pot and Stalin. However, it was this bloodthirsty prince, enemy of the Ottoman Empire, whom the Muses chose for a literary destiny.

In 1897, the Irishman Bram Stoker, secretary and tour manager of the great actor Henry Irving, allowed himself to be tempted by the pen and, inspired by a vampire story conjured up by his compatriot Sheridan Le Fanu, published a ghastly novel whose protagonist is a Victorian version of the Wallachian prince, who now, instead of impaling his victims, bites them. The imperious Draculesti, in his adopted Hungarian nationality and reduced to the first three syllables of his name, has carried since Stoker's days the most Gothic attributes of fear: blood, tombs, night, cold, bats, fangs, and a black cape. Above all, blood.

The story Stoker made up for him is bloody in every sense. There is the aristocratic blood that runs through the ancient count's veins and the blood the anemic creature must drink night after night; there is (implicitly) the blood of Our Redeemer mocked by the satanic rituals of the vampire and the blood of political power fed by the plebeian blood of the middle class born of the Industrial Revolution. And in the cartography of the human body, there is the subcutaneous blood whose exit point towards the outside world—the fountain's mouth, the vital spout, the echo chamber of orgasm—is in the neck.

Dracula's story is a story of necks. The neck is the stage on which Stoker's drama takes place: the necks of somnambular women dressed in translucent negligees, the proud necks of those who oppose the Count, the brave necks stuck out by those who pursue him, the virgin necks of his innocent victims. In absolute terms, what is the neck's attraction? Shakespeare's contemporary Maurice Scève declared that the Creator, in order not to restrict beauty to the "tiny realm" of the face, extended it to the ivory neck that Scève calls "a branch, a column of the altar, a lectern for Venus's letters, a tallboy of chastity."

But why, of all the bits and pieces of the human body, should this singular region, the obligatory passage from the torso to the head, be the one to attract the seducer's lips, the assassin's hands, the executioner's ax, the monster's fangs? What does the nakedness of this delicate and sensitive area have, for it to draw upon itself the heat of erotic violence, or of violence *tout court?* Perhaps because it is there, more than in other parts of the body, that the skin barely conceals the web of veins and secret arteries, the vampire, like an explorer of a wondrous hidden world, curious to discover the subterranean realm that might lead to the essence of our being, daringly seeks to enter that mysterious undergrowth, tangled, dark, and forbidden. Knowing himself ultimately condemned, like all of us, to death, Count Dracula seeks the source of life.

Above adolescent dreams hovers now the shadow of the somber Count, because in that change from childhood to adulthood, adolescents long for, and fear, the initiation to the infamous acts of their elders. Above the dreams of the old it hovers as well, because at the end of our lives we wish for what is irretrievable: the touch of firm skin, the warmth of young lips, the beating of hot blood. Somewhere in his lengthy poem on the Rose, Jean de Meung suggested that the fountain of youth is not of water but of blood.

Apostle of blood, lord of the night, invader of sleep in the privacy of the bedroom, in spite of being destined to the tomb, Count Dracula cannot die. Against this interdiction are useless the tricks of Dr. Van Helsing, the conclusion decreed by the author of the novel, the crucifixes and the garlic, the parodies and satires that pretend not to fear him, the severity of scientific laws that repudiate the certainty of his existence. In spite of all this, again and again, Count Dracula returns. The aliases provided for him by novelists and filmmakers, the new adventures imagined by Anne Rice and Stephenie Meyer, the various features lent to him by Max von Schreck, Bela Lugosi, and Tom Cruise are of no avail. We must resign ourselves to the fact that Count Dracula has become, in our bleak age, a necessary monster.

ALICE

Of all the miracles that pinpoint the histories of our literatures, few are as miraculous as that of the birth of Alice. On the afternoon of July 4, 1862, the reverend Charles Lutwidge Dodgson, accompanied by a friend, took the three young daughters of Dr. Liddell, Dean of Christ Church, on a three-mile boating expedition up the Thames near Oxford. The girls demanded a story and the Reverend Dodgson began improvising one about his favorite friend, the seven-year-old Alice. "Sometimes to

tease us," Alice Liddell recalled years later, "Mr. Dodgson would stop suddenly and say, 'And that's all till next time.' 'Ah, but it is next time,' would be the exclamation from all three: and after some persuasion the story would start afresh." When they returned, Alice asked Dodgson to write out the story for her. He said he would try, and sat up nearly the whole night putting it down on paper, and gave the story the title of *Alice's Adventures Underground*. Three years later, in 1865, the story was published by Macmillan in London under the pseudonym "Lewis Carroll" and the title *Alice's Adventures in Wonderland*.

That Alice's adventures were invented while the excursion proceeded is almost unbelievable. That Alice's fall and explorations, her encounters and her discoveries, the syllogisms and puns and wise jokes, should, in all their fantastic and coherent development have been made up then and there, in the telling, seems truly miraculous. No miracle, however, is entirely inexplicable, and it may be that Alice's tale has deeper roots than its nursery reputation might suggest.

The Alice books have never been read like other children's stories. Their geography has the powerful reverberations of certain mythical places, such as Utopia or Arcadia. In the *Commedia,* the guardian spirit on the summit of Mount Purgatory explains to Dante that the Golden Age of which poets have sung is an unconscious memory of Paradise Lost, of a vanished state of perfect happiness; perhaps Wonderland is the unconscious memory of a state of perfect reason, a state which, seen now through the eyes of social and cultural conventions, appears to us as utter madness. Whoever follows Alice down the rabbit hole and through the Red Queen's labyrinthine kingdom, and later through the looking-glass, never does it for the first time. Only the Liddell sisters can be said to have been present at the creation, and even then, they must have had a sense of déjà vu: after that first day, Wonderland and the Chess Kingdom entered the universal library much like the Garden of Eden, a place which we know exists without ever having set foot in it. The geography of Alice (though it is not on any map; "real places never are," as Melville noted) is the recurrent landscape of our dream life.

Because the world of Alice is, of course, our world: not in abstract symbolic terms, not as a calculated allegory, not as a dystopian fable. Wonderland is simply the mad place in which we find ourselves daily, with its quotidian ration of the heavenly, the hellish, and the purgatorial— a place through which we must wander as we wander through life. Alice (like us) is armed with only one weapon for the journey: language. It is with words that we make our way through the Cheshire Cat's forest and the Queen of Hearts' croquet ground. It is with words that Alice discovers the difference between what things are and what they appear to be. It is her questioning that brings out the madness of Wonderland, hidden, as in our world, under a thin coat of conventional respectability. We may try to find logic in madness, as the Duchess does by finding a moral to everything, however absurd, but the truth is, as the Cheshire Cat tells Alice, that we have no choice in the matter: whichever path we follow, we will find ourselves among mad people, and we must use language as best we can to keep a grip on what we deem to be our sanity. Words reveal to Alice (and to us) that the only indisputable fact of this bewildering world is that under an apparent rationality we are all mad. Like Alice, we risk drowning ourselves and everyone else in our own tears. We like to think, as the Dodo does, that no matter in what direction or how incompetently we run, we should all be winners and we should all be entitled to a prize. Like the White Rabbit, we give orders left and right, as if others should feel obliged (and honored) to serve us. Like the Caterpillar, we question the identity of our fellow creatures but have little idea of our own, even on the verge of losing that identity. We believe, like the Duchess, in punishment for the annoying behavior of the young, but have little interest in the reasons for that behavior. Like the Mad Hatter, we feel that we alone have the right to food and drink at a table set for many more, and we cynically offer the thirsty and hungry wine when there is no wine and jam every day except today. Under the rule of despots like the Queen of Hearts, we are forced to play mad games with inadequate instruments— balls that roll away like hedgehogs and sticks that twist and turn like live flamingoes—and when we are unable to follow the instructions, we are threatened with having our heads chopped off. Our education methods, as the Gryphon and the Mock Turtle explain to Alice, are either exercises in nostalgia (the teaching of Laughing and Grief) or training courses in the service of others (how to be thrown with the lobsters into sea). And our system of justice, long before Kafka described it, is like the one set up to judge the Knave of Hearts, incomprehensible and unfair. Few of us, however, have Alice's courage, at the end of the first book, to stand up (literally) for our convictions and refuse to hold our tongue. Because of this supreme act of civil disobedience, Alice is allowed to wake from her dream. We, of course, are not.

Fellow voyagers, we recognize in Alice's journey the themes ever present in our lives: pursuit and loss of dreams, the attendant tears and suffering, the race for survival, being forced into servitude, the nightmare of confused self-identity, the effects of dysfunctional families, the required submission to nonsensical arbitration, the abuse of authority, perverted teaching, the impotent knowledge of unpunished crimes and unfair punishments, and the long struggle of reason against unreason. All this, and the pervading sense of madness, are, in fact, a summary of the Alice books themselves.

"To define true madness," we are told in *Hamlet,* "what is't but to be nothing else but mad?" Alice would have agreed: madness is the exclusion of everything that is not mad and therefore everyone in Wonderland falls under the Cheshire Cat's dictum. But Alice is not Hamlet. Her dreams are not bad dreams; she never mopes, she never sees herself as the hand of ghostly justice, she never insists on proof of what is crystal clear, she believes in immediate action. Words, for Alice, are not simply words but living creatures, and thinking does not make things good or bad. She certainly does not want her solid flesh to melt, anymore than she wants it to shoot up or shrink down (even though, in order to pass through the small garden door, she wishes she could "shut up like a telescope"). Alice would never have succumbed to a poisoned blade or drunk, like Hamlet's mother, from a poisoned cup: picking up the bottle that says "DRINK ME" she first looks to see whether it is marked *poison* or not, "for she had read several nice little stories about children who had got burnt, and eaten up by wild beasts, and other unpleasant things, all because they *would* not remember the simple rules their friends had taught them." Alice is much more reasonable than the Prince of Denmark.

Like Hamlet, however, Alice must have wondered, crammed inside the White Rabbit's house, if she too might not be bounded in a nutshell, but as to being king (or queen) of infinite space, Alice does not merely fret about it: she strives for the title and, in *Through the Looking-Glass,* she works hard to earn the promised dream-crown. Alice, brought up on strict Victorian precepts rather than lax Elizabethan ones, believes in discipline and tradition, and has no time for grumbling and procrastination. Throughout her adventures Alice, like a well-brought-up child, confronts unreason with simple logic. Convention (the artificial construct of reality) is set against fantasy (the natural reality). Alice knows instinctively that logic is our way of making sense of nonsense and uncovering its secret rules, and she applies it ruthlessly, even among her elders and betters, whether confronting the Duchess or the Mad Hatter. And when arguments prove useless, she insists on at least making the unjust absurdity of the situation plain. When the Queen of Hearts demands that the court should give the "sentence first—verdict afterwards," Alice quite rightly answers, "Stuff and nonsense!" That is the only answer that most of the absurdities in our world deserve.

And yet, in spite of its apparent madness, like that of

Wonderland, our world tantalizingly suggests that it *does* have a meaning and that if we look hard enough behind the "stuff and nonsense" we will find something that explains it all. Alice's adventures proceed with uncanny precision and coherence, so that we, as readers, have the growing impression of an elusive sense in all the nonsense. The entire book has the quality of a Zen koan or a Greek paradox, of something meaningful and at the same time inexplicable, something on the verge of revelation. What we feel, falling down the rabbit hole after Alice and following her through her journey, is that Wonderland's madness is not arbitrary, nor is it innocent. Half epic and half dream, Lewis Carroll's invention lays out for us a necessary space somewhere between solid earth and fairyland, a vantage point from which to see the universe in more or less explicit terms, translated, as it were, into a story. Like the mathematical formulas that fascinated the Reverend Dodgson, Alice's adventures are both hard fact and lofty invention. They exist on two planes simultaneously: one which grounds us in the reality of flesh and blood, and one upon which that reality can be reconsidered and transformed, like the Cheshire Cat perched on its branch, drifting from something bewilderingly visible to the miraculous (and reassuring) ghost of a smile.

FAUST

Dr. Faust (or Faustus) is old, Dr. Faust is nostalgic. The latter is a consequence of the former: the longings of youth are for time future, never time past. What the doctor seeks is what he has lost, or believes he has lost, in the distant days when he was a young man. This is what Christopher Marlowe imagined in 1604 and then what Goethe imagined further two centuries later. Faust wants to be granted the prerogatives of elderly knowledge at the same time he enjoys those of young love: a double-edged

miracle that his assistant Wagner calls "illumination."
"Sweet moment, don't vanish!" he begs of this miraculous
alliance in the words Goethe gave him. To achieve this
illumination of erotic wisdom, human science seems to
Faust inadequate, and he seeks assistance in the science of
magic. Then, as we know from the story, Mephistopheles
appears.

Mephistopheles (Goethe's version of the devil) defines
himself as a failure, someone who wishes to do evil but,
much to his regret, does good. He wants to be absolutely
wicked but Something or Someone constantly stands
in his way, and his devilish plots and strategies do not
achieve the desired effect. This is one of the most curious
traits of Mephistopheles. We think that evil must almost
always be victorious and offer as proof the great and small
miseries of our daily life, and the horrors and infamies
of our common histories. But for Mephistopheles, who
should know about these things, that is not so. In spite
of all human suffering, good seems to triumph in the
end. Mephistopheles, like Barbara Cartland, believes that
everything, in spite of his efforts, has a happy ending and,
curiously enough, he is mostly right. Though in Marlowe's *Doctor Faustus* the flames of hell devour the greedy
doctor (who, like a coward, offers to burn his books if he
is saved, as if the poor things were guilty of his ambition),
the First Part of Goethe's *Faust* concludes with the salvation of Gretchen, the young woman whom Faust has
seduced, and the Second Part with the sinful doctor's
own. These failed attempts at doing evil are perhaps to
blame for Mephistopheles' bad reputation. "From hero

to general, from general to politician, from politician to secret service agent, and thence to a thing that peers in at bedroom or bathroom windows, and thence to a toad, and finally to a snake—such is the progress of Satan," wrote C. S. Lewis in his "Preface" to Milton's *Paradise Lost*.

But the doctor is insistent. That is how Thomas Mann understood it when, under the pen name of Adrian Leverkühn, he had Faust accept once more the terrible and inefficient bond. By way of the failed poet Enoch Soames, Max Beerbohm suggested a sardonic British take on the tragedy. Via Gounod's opera, the Argentinian poet Estanislao del Campo created a gaucho who tells of the drama he has just heard sung onstage. In the midst of Stalin's horrors, Mikhail Bulgakov dreamt up a dark Russian interpretation of the pact, *The Master and Margarita*. One of the earliest versions is the anonymous *Story of Doctor Faustus* that appeared in print in Germany in 1587; innumerable editions followed, including one made into a puppet show that Goethe saw as a child, which no doubt fed his adult nightmares.

In past centuries, when trading one's soul was considered an earth-shattering undertaking, things were easier for Mephistopheles, whether he came out a winner or not. Nowadays, when the soul holds for us infinitely less prestige, and when every day we exchange our souls for trinkets such as a pipeline contract or a seat in the Senate, Mephistopheles' task is, paradoxically, much more difficult. To lose one's soul in exchange for a trinket lends the soul the value of a trinket, and Mephistopheles (whose natural business is usury) longs for what is precious. Because the

Fausts of today seek not knowledge and love but financial gain, an invitation to a reality show, their name in digital lights, Mephistopheles has to work ten times as hard to amass the necessary number of souls to make a profit.

GERTRUDE

She thinks, The boy has issues. He's no longer a surly, grumpy, malicious adolescent, rude to his elders, "fat, and scant of breath." Now he's a surly, grumpy, malicious adult, rude to his elders, "fat, and scant of breath." As a mother she finds this hard to admit, but she thinks her son is not quite right in the head. As a boy he played with imaginary friends; now he sees ghosts and dreams of dark plots and weird conspiracies. Perhaps the boredom of life at court (in Denmark, no less, where for six months of

the year it's bedtime) has led him to make up cloak-and-dagger stories. Maybe he had grown too accustomed to amusing philosophical banter and frothy muscular beer at his German university. He thinks too much, that's his problem. He needs to go out more, play sports, hunt seals, take a swim in the freezing waters of Elsinore like all the other young men his age, run after girls. He is driving poor Ophelia crazy with a yes, a no, a let's wait and see, forcing old Polonius, who after all has certain obligations as a parent, to ask what the Prince's intentions are. He only seems happy (well, *happy* is too strong a term—less melancholy) when he is with other young men, such as Horatio and that lot, and those other two boys, so nicely groomed and well behaved, Rosencrantz and Guilden-stern, as inseparable (Hamlet says) as Achilles and Patroclus. And also with that bunch of actors dressed in women's clothes, putting on little avant-garde plays in the dining room of the palace. Maybe he's gay. That would explain his annoying "To be or not to be." Gertrude wishes he would make up his mind. For God's sake, he wouldn't be the only gay man in the court of Elsinore.

Being a mother is always difficult, but with an only son who's always moping about, there are times when Gertrude wishes she could take a long, long holiday somewhere warm and sunny. Why, she wonders, is she always saddled with sad, whiny men? Her late husband would wake up every morning pale and grumbling, and go to bed every night sighing deeply, with "a counte-nance more in sorrow than in anger," as Horatio cau-tiously puts it. He can't have been much fun. And her second husband, Claudius? Hamlet (prejudiced, of course) calls him a toad, a bat, a tomcat that rolls about in "an enseamèd bed / Stewed in corruption." At the same time (explain this, says Gertrude), Hamlet imagines that "mildewed ear" as a sort of gallant Menelaus willing to kill for the love of Helen. Claudius a gallant? Are we serious?

And then there's Hamlet himself.

The question that no one dares ask is this: Did Gertrude really want to be a mother? Maybe she is more like Lady Macbeth, willing to pluck her nipple from her child's boneless gums and dash its brains out, or like Medea, unflinchingly stabbing her two children to spite her husband, or like Sarah Jeanette Duncan's heroine in *A Mother in India* who believes that the obligation of motherhood is a notion promoted by men because, as she says, "Men are very slow in changing their philosophy about women. I fancy their idea of the maternal relation is firmest fixed of all." Torvald, Nora's husband in Ibsen's *A Doll's House,* argues that "almost everyone who has turned out bad early in life, has had a deceitful mother." Is, then, Hamlet's obnoxious behavior all Gertrude's fault?

Who is Gertrude?

We don't know. Doubtless she is the daughter of kings, wife of kings, destined to be mother of a king and presumably (if Hamlet ever gets going) grandmother of kings. Gertrude lacks an individual, self-serving function. Her role is to depend on others, to exist subservient to others. When Hamlet stages the play that with heavy-handed symbolism he calls *The Mousetrap* in order to make Claudius confess to the murder, and Claudius, frightened (or perhaps fed up with the experimental performance), stops the play, we learn nothing of Gertrude's sentiments except that she's concerned about Claudius.

But what must Gertrude have felt, not at seeing the silly staging of the presumed crime, but about the image her deluded son so obviously has of her? The dream life of Hamlet mingles with the other, the daily life to which Gertrude is forever condemned. It denies the patience with which she has had to gird herself in order to endure the weariness of the days and nights of Elsinore, denies the strategies she has had to devise to overcome the injustices she has suffered because of her sex and rank, denies her any small victories over the miseries of life, denies her the consolation of hope redefined at every successive moment. John Locke described the self (it could be Gertrude's) as an empty darkened room through which reality enters only through a pinhole in the wall. Gertrude does not even have the right to that pinhole.

Gertrude wishes for things to be different, for her obligations to be excused, for the rules of the game to be other. When the deaths of which Hamlet is guilty begin to pile up ("One woe doth tread upon another's heel" is how she sums things up), Gertrude, tired of so many executed innocents and so many ambiguous executioners, begins to feel something like envy. That is why, in the last moments, when Claudius begs her not to drink from the cup he knows is poisoned, Gertrude insists, "I will, my lord; I pray you pardon me." This "pardon me" is one of the most moving lines in the play, a plea that unfortunately, in the thud of tumbling bodies and the trumpeting of pompous last words, is barely discernable. Only later, once the whole thing is over, does there hang in the rank air a vague, uncanny, persistent echo of her ironic farewell. Because in the ghostly castle of Elsinore, Gertrude's ghost is the only uncontrovertibly true one.

SUPERMAN

I first met Superman in 1960 when I was twelve. I had been taken by my nanny to Baltimore for a six-month holiday. There I discovered many wonders: baloney sandwiches, square-bottomed brown paper bags that served admirably to make Halloween masks, the erotically charged pocket book racks in the corner drugstore, Bazooka bubble gum in its lurid cartoon wrapper, *Boris Karloff Presents* on late-night TV, and the Baltimore Stock Exchange, to which my nanny's brother took me one

bewildering morning. But the main delights were the American comic book heroes: Batman and his beloved Robin, Little Lulu and fat Toby, the bone-tingling mad scientists of *Tales of the Crypt,* Wonder Woman with her gaucho boots and silver lasso. And of course, Superman, the Man of Steel, his inamorata Lois Lane, his buddy Jimmy Olsen, and his archenemy, Lex Luthor.

In Argentina, we had versions of most of these comic books translated into Spanish in Mexico and therefore known as *revistas mexicanas.* Because their heroes were so obviously foreign, they did not truly compete with our homegrown characters, such as Patorozú, the super-strong *indio,* and El Eternauta, the traveler who arrived in Buenos Aires from the distant future. But they had the appeal of exotic, colorful ambassadors from the mysterious North.

I felt a kinship with Superman. Not, of course, because of his superpowers but because of his forced isolation and sense of exclusion. Launched into space by parents who wanted to save him from the destruction of their planet, adopted by a farming couple who instill in him fundamental civic virtues, obliged to lead the double life of a timid newspaper reporter who is secretly a powerful hero, Superman had many of the features of a less than confident adolescent with an overpowering literary passion of which he felt vaguely guilty.

From our earliest histories, we have enjoyed imagining supermen of all sorts. Enkidu, Gilgamesh's eventual partner, is so strong that he can kill the wild bull of Ishtar; Heracles fulfills twelve seemingly impossible tasks; Nimrod, the great-grandson of Noah, is "a mighty hunter before the Lord," and uses his strength to build the Tower of Babel in order to fight the Lord's hosts in heaven; Samson, "eyeless in Gaza, at the mill with slaves," as Milton puts it, has his strength divinely restored so that he can pull down the columns of the temple of Dagon and kill both himself and his captors in one of the earliest recorded suicide attacks; the giant lumberjack Paul Bunyan who roamed the American Midwest with his pet blue ox Babe was supposed to be seven feet tall and have a stride of over three yards.

In the first years of the twentieth century, George Bernard Shaw dreamed up a version of the Superman in his play about Don Juan. "We must either breed political capacity," Shaw wrote in the preface, "or be ruined by Democracy, which was forced on us by the failure of the older alternatives. Yet if Despotism failed only for want of a capable benevolent despot, what chance has Democracy, which requires a whole population of capable voters." Shaw's friend and opponent G. K. Chesterton intuited a deeper truth in the Superman: an inhuman and preternatural fragility. Going to meet the marvelous creature, Chesterton asks the Superman's parents whether he is handsome. "He creates his own standard," the parents reply. "Upon that plane he is more than Apollo. Seen from our lower plane, of course . . ." "Has he got any hair?" Chesterton asks. "Everything upon that plane is different," they answer. "What he has got is not . . . well, not, of course, what we call hair . . . but . . ." "Well, what on earth is it," Chesterton asks with some irritation, "if it isn't hair? Is it feathers?" "Not feathers, as we understand feathers." Unable to contain his curiosity, Chesterton rushes into the room that houses the indescribable creature. From the darkness comes a small sad yelp. "You have done it, now!" his parents cry. "You have let in a draught on him; and he is dead."

Chesterton saw his Superman as an all-ailing weakling. Other supermen also have their weak spots, which, in the eyes of their admirers, somehow make their superhuman power even more admirable. To avoid losing his strength, Samson must not cut his hair, Achilles must protect his celebrated heel, Heracles must cast off the poisoned shirt of Nessus. Superman is sensitive to kryptonite, the mineral ejected from his planet at the time of its explosion,. Kryptonite has different and awful effects on our hero, depending on its color: green, red, or gold. The worst is green kryptonite, which saps Superman of his strength and leaves him in a kind of immune-deficiency condition.

Nietzsche had his Zarathustra extol the virtues of the Superman (the clumsy English translation of the German *Übermensch*) as one who is powerful because he seeks human virtues on earth and not in any kind of hopeful afterlife. For Nietzsche, the Superman is anything but the idealistic, liberal, justice-seeking humanitarian of the future Marvel comics. On the contrary, Nietzsche's Superman opposes the concepts of "modern, good and Christian men and other nihilists" and embraces those of an all-mighty male individual. Because for Nietzsche there is no Superwoman: the duty of women, according to Nietzsche, is to give birth to the Supermen. "When I whispered into the ears of some people," Nietzsche wrote in *Ecce Homo*, "that they were better off looking for a

Cesare Borgia than a Parsifal, they did not believe their ears." Nietzsche's Superman is closer to Lex Luthor than to the Man of Steel.

Fact-checking readers at Harvard University have looked for (and found) a number of physical impossibilities in the admired superhuman abilities granted to the hero by his creators, Jerry Siegel and Joe Shuster, since his appearance in the first issue of *Action Comics* on April 18, 1938. For instance, Superman's X-ray vision. Even if he truly had the ability to produce a chemical reaction capable of shooting X-rays out of his eyes, these inquisitors say, the rays would still have to bounce off an appropriate surface in order to get back to Superman's photoreceptors and enable him to see the captured image, not to mention the risk of cancer that a double exposure of X-rays would cause in any living creature inspected by the Man of Steel.

Superman's invulnerability has also been poohpoohed. To protect him from slings, arrows, and atomic weapons, Siegel and Shuster lent him a very thin aura of some sort that surrounds him at all times, so that while his cape might get shredded in his many passionate adventures, his suit never tears to expose his naked sexy body. The same inquisitors have suggested that this aura is a non-Newtonian fluid—that is to say, a fluid much like custard that does not follow Newton's law of viscosity and can change when under force, becoming either more liquid or more solid. To prove or disprove this theory, the inquisitors have called for volunteers to lick the Man of Steel and see if he tastes sweet.

In an episode of the television show *The Big Bang*

Theory, the scientifically minded Sheldon seeks to debunk Superman's ability to catch falling bodies in flight. "Lois Lane," he suggests, "is falling, accelerating at an initial rate of 32 feet per second per second. Superman swoops down to save her by reaching out two arms of steel. Miss Lane, who is now traveling at approximately 120 miles per hour, hits them, and is immediately sliced into three equal pieces." And he adds: "If he really loved her, he'd let her hit the pavement. It would be a more merciful death."

In spite of the apparent impossibilities inherent to his nature, in spite of growing competition from other younger heroes and heroines, in spite of a changing world in which villains no longer assume astute disguises to conduct their evil business, Superman's appeal has not diminished.

A few years ago, the poet Dorianne Laux wrote an elegy, portraying Superman dying of what is probably kryptonite cancer:

> It's 2010 and the doctors have given him
> another year in Metropolis. Another year
> in paradise when he's high, another year
> in hell when he's not.
> A magazine falls from his lap. Lois
> on the cover of *Fortune,* the planets
> aligned behind her, starlight glancing off
> her steely upswept hair.

DON JUAN

To systematize pleasure, to submit it to a routine of conquests, to turn the beloved's name into a checked item on a list of things to do, is a fairly effective way of warding off amorous passion. Don Juan is less a lover than a seducer, less a seducer than a collector, less a collector than a sniper. Other donjuanesque characters seem to have a clear purpose in their erotic campaigns—many times an evil one, as in the case of the loathsome Valmont

in *Les Liaisons dangereuses* and of the dark protagonists of Sade's fables. Not so Don Juan: his is a perfect *acte gratuit*. We are not even certain that this celebrated lover ever achieved physical pleasure. Seemingly he finds it enough to add another name to his catalogue of conquests without telling us if the deed has granted him more than a statistical victory. "But, alas, I tire in vain / of throwing punches in the air," he says in Tirso de Molina's seventeenth-century *Trickster of Seville,* echoing Onan's ancient complaint. His is an accounting obsession, not an erotic one: Mercury claims him, not Cupid. He wants to gather women as others gather stocks. Molière says that for Don Juan, "all the pleasure of love subsists in change." The ladies' names in his cabinet of curiosities replace the unicorn's horn and the bezoar stone that his contemporaries lust for.

It is not even the essential woman that he desires: not her soul, her personality, her secret identity; he wants merely her public persona, her social status, her typological traits. In Tirso's version, the list of his victims includes the aristocratic Isabella, the fisherwoman Tisbea, the noble Donna Ana, the rustic Aminta. The catalogue recited by the hero's servant, Leporello, in Mozart and Da Ponte's *Don Giovanni* is even longer. In the nineteenth century, José Zorrilla, in his *Don Juan Tenorio,* makes these strategies explicit:

> Into grand palaces I went,
> Of humble huts I had the key,
> And everywhere I left behind
> Infamous memories of me.

Words that would not be out of place on the tongues of the Spanish conquistadores plundering the realms of the New World . . .

But not everything in the Don Juan story is mere listing. We feel that in spite of his boasting, there is more to his strife than the banal wish to collect by any means available the largest possible number of female specimens. "'Tis sweet to win, no matter how, one's laurels," Don Juan declares in Byron's poem. And yet, another obsession, darker and more disturbing, seems to animate our hero. Perhaps because his reputation is that of a seducer, a meticulous hunter, we forget that Don Juan is also an adventurer in the kingdom of the dead, a man capable of conversing with ghosts, like Odysseus and Aeneas and Dante before him.

Even in the midst of his plots, Don Juan knows that, when all is said and done, none of his undertakings will come to a happy conclusion. Convinced, like Mallarmé, that "all flesh is sad" (even though he might not have read all the books) Don Juan understands that every amorous conquest must resolve itself in the same unhappy state, and so he seeks a more positive resolution with the only lover who cannot be unfaithful. Let us not forget that Don Juan's mother tongue is Spanish, and that in Spanish (as in French and Italian, unlike English and German) Death is feminine. That is why Don Juan summons the ghost of the Comendador to a last supper, knowing for certain that she will also attend and that he, like a true gentleman, will offer to accompany her home.

LiLiTH

According to a Jewish legend of the early Middle Ages, before fashioning Eve out of Adam's rib, God created an earlier woman to keep Adam company during the long hours in the Garden. To this precursor of Eve, God gave the name Lilith.

What pleases Lilith most is realizing that she is indispensable. If you are going to have creation, you cannot do without her. She is the ear that allows the mouth to

speak, the eyes that reflect back sight, the shadow that proves the existence of the sun, the second player who lends meaning to the first. As Lilith knows well, every birth implies an end, every assertion calls for questioning, every settlement demands a disruption. From the moment of creation itself, definition is separation, and therefore it cries out to its lost half: "Who am I?" That is a question Lilith is prepared to answer, and not with apologetic meekness or riddling self-defeating haughtiness. When Lilith tells us who she is, her answer will not be an onomastic mask or a pompous "I am what I am."

Like everything else, Lilith once existed deep within the dark void of earth and sea. Then the Spirit moved on the face of the waters and Lilith knew that her time had come. The darkness sent forth the light to reveal itself, the formless earth bred living creatures to discover its destined shape, the One God created an image of himself and held it in his palm to inspect it. Everything else was fashioned from the word of God; only his image (whom God called Adam) was made by his hand. Then, because God likes symmetry, he scooped up a handful of dust to make a companion for Adam. This is how Lilith came into the world. Dust blows in the wind and takes on new shapes, and never settles for long in one place; the nature of Lilith was therefore changeable, and she delighted in trying out numberless faces and bodies. There was never just one Lilith. So much is clear.

Because Adam was made in God's image, Adam was also an image of the permanence of the world, since God is, by definition, unchanging. The hair upon God's head is like a forest, his tears are like a river, his mouth is like an ocean. Every part of his body is also an image of the world. The ball of his eye has the shape of the earth, the white of his eye is like the ocean that circles the earth, Jerusalem is the pupil and the Temple the reflection in the pupil. This Adam believed, in spite of Lilith's cautions. "There is more to all this than a game of shifting mirrors," she would tell him. But Adam refused to listen or to ask why. As Lilith knew, everything carries a purpose: wind ministers to God, fire to the angels, and water to the demons. Earth nourishes the animals, and the animals obey man. "And all of them serve Lilith," Lilith concluded, but not aloud. "Including Adam."

Of Lilith's sojourn with Adam, there is little to say beyond the story told in the Midrash. God had created a garden expressly for them, with four magical rivers and many bountiful trees, and marvelous beasts of every kind. A few laws ruled the garden, such as not wading into the rivers' waters or slaughtering the animals, and, above all, not eating from the fruit of the Tree of Life, which rose in the garden's very center. For a time, Lilith tried coaxing Adam into adventurous deeds, daring enterprises, new forms of thinking. Adam refused, partly because he loved immutability and partly because he resented being told what to do. What he enjoyed most was standing among the newly invented creatures and giving them names. He called the horse "horse" and the dog "dog" and the many-colored beast whose skin served to clothe the Tabernacle "tahash," and the dolphins who have sexual intercourse with humans "sons of the sea." Lilith would take on the shape of these beings and try to show Adam what they really were, but Adam paid no attention to her and preferred to rely on the truth of the letters of the alphabet, which reveal the veritable essence of that which they name. "The alphabet was there before the world began," he would say to her, and turn away.

By taking on the shape of God's created beings, Lilith became friendly with many of the beasts and chatted with them for hours since in those days all beings spoke the same language. Some of the beasts she liked for their natural wit and courage, and she pranced among them in the guise of a panther or a long-horned bull; others she despised for their stupidity or their meekness. It is said that in later times, it was Lilith who slew Job's oxen and asses.

Best-beloved of Lilith was the serpent, whose qualities, God had decided, most resembled those of Adam. Like Adam, the serpent stood upright upon two feet, tall as a camel; like Adam, it had fine intellectual qualities and the ability to reflect on intellectual problems; like Adam, it was gifted with craftsmanship; it made wonderful objects of gold and silver, and knew the secrets of gems and pearls. When Lilith took on the shape of the serpent, they would spend long hours together, deep in conversation, or busy fashioning intricate jewels that Lilith would then offer to God when he walked in the Garden in the cool of the day. God found them pleasingly beautiful.

Lilith and the serpent conversed often, and Adam began to feel left out. "I have not given you permission to spend the afternoon in the serpent's company," he would say to Lilith. Or, "I expect you to remain by my side in case I require your services." But Lilith would pay no attention to his commands, and Adam complained to God. "She is willful, she is disobedient, she refuses to stay still. She is a never-silent bell. I'm afraid that she may even ignore your prohibitions, and I won't be held accountable for what may happen then."

In spite of Adam's recriminations, Lilith and the serpent continued to converse. "Do you know why God wants you to obey Adam?" the serpent asked Lilith, "and why he forbids Adam to eat from the fruit of the Tree? Artisans of the same guild hate one another (this was to be written out later in the Talmud) and he alone wants to have the power to create and destroy."

Lilith remained with Adam for as long as she could bear it, and then disappeared. For a time, Adam mistook her for the serpent, whose shape she had so often assumed, and when he saw it curled in the branches of a tree, legs tucked neatly beneath its long body, he thought: "Let her be, she'll soon be tired of her game and she'll become a woman again."

At length, the truth was discovered. Furious at her insolence, God sent three angels after her. They found her in the Red Sea, where she had bred a nestful of demons, born perhaps from her liaison with the serpent (the Midrash is doubtful about this, though cautiously tells us that no one must ever drink from its waters). Sternly, the angels said to Lilith that unless she flew back with them to rejoin Adam, a hundred of her demon children would be killed every day. Lilith replied that she preferred this punishment to returning to Adam and being his slave.

Now Lilith takes her revenge by injuring baby boys

on the first night of their life, and girls until their twentieth day. Lilith's powers are at their height whenever the moon turns red. The only way to ward her off is to tie to the child's wrist an amulet bearing the names of the three pursuing angels. This too is in the Midrash.

THE WANDERING JEW

During his painful path along the Via Dolorosa, the
wooden cross and the bloody lashes of the Roman guards
on his shoulders, mocked and jeered by the crowd, Jesus
felt thirsty and stopped at a fountain for a sip of water. An
old Jew pushed him away and told him to keep on going.
"I will go," Jesus answered him, "but you will wait until
I come back." Then he continued on his way to Mount
Golgotha. Thus was born the medieval legend of the Wandering Jew. His great sin is having offended the Son of

God; his punishment, to wander until the end of time because for the Word of God to be fulfilled Jesus will not return until the Day of Judgment.

In the Gospel of John (18:20–22) it is told that when the Roman soldiers came to arrest Jesus, one of them slapped him in the face: perhaps this scene inspired the story, which has, of course, no biblical authority. In any case, it took some twelve hundred years for the legend to develop fully, during which time the anonymous Jew acquired a number of different names. Some are mysterious, such as Cartaphilus and Ahasverus, others explicit, such as Buttadeus ("Shove-God" in Portuguese) and Juan-Espera-en-Dios ("John-Who-Waits-for-God" in Spanish). The seventeenth-century Jesuit Baltasar Gracián attempted to be explicit and called him Juan-de-Para-Siempre, "John-for-All-Time."

Beginning in the thirteenth century a handful of witnesses started to appear in support of the story. A Bolognese chronicler of the thirteenth century noted that in 1223, Emperor Frederick II heard from the lips of a couple of pilgrims that they had met a Jew in Armenia who was the very one Jesus had condemned to be a traveler throughout eternity. The English historian Roger of Wendover, in a chronicle written in 1228, affirms that this same Jew, interviewed by the archbishop of Armenia, confessed that in days long past he had been in the employ of Pontius Pilate. A few decades later, Matthew Paris, in his *Chronica Major,* tells the same story and adds that the Jew had now repented and said that he had put his trust in God's divine mercy. On June 9, 1564, the anonymous author of *Short Description and Account of a Jew Named Ahasverus* swore that he had seen the Wandering Jew in Schleswig. He described him as a tall man with long hair and calloused soles two inches thick who spoke fluent Spanish because he had lived for a time in Madrid. Some of these chronicles grant the Jew a wife and several children who accompany him on his journeys.

Closer to our day, the story was developed further by dozens of different writers, among whom the best known are Eugène Sue (who links the Jew to Jesuit plots), Pär Lagerkvist (who sees him as a unrecognized prophet), Mark Twain (for whom the Jew is just another banal tourist), and Jorge Luis Borges (who wove the Jew's story together with that of an immortal Homer). James Joyce gave him the name Leopold Bloom and forced him to wander through the city of Dublin for a full day that becomes eternal. The editorial team of Carlo Fruttero and Franco Lucentini conceived him as a middle-aged man with no fixed abode, working as a tourist guide in Venice, surely an eternal city if there ever was one.

Leaving aside the obvious anti-Semitism of the legend, the notion of travel as punishment is a curious one, though it appears in other stories. In that of *The Flying Dutchman,* for example, the cursed captain of the wandering vessel is supposed to be in league with the devil. For Sir Walter Scott, *The Flying Dutchman* was a pirate ship "loaded with great wealth, on board of which some horrid act of murder and piracy had been committed." Robert Louis Stevenson, blissfully unaware of the hysteria of airports and security regulations of today, argued that "to travel hopefully is a better thing than to arrive," and would not have agreed that the peregrinations of either

The Flying Dutchman or the Wandering Jew were to be understood as punishments. To travel the world, to see exotic landscapes, to discover other peoples and customs are activities that, beyond the charm of being adventurous, have always been recommended as the best education possible, both for the devotees of expensive ocean cruises and for the risk-taking penny-pinching users of Airbnb.

However, there is a darker side to this Stevensonian notion of travel, perhaps the one imagined by Jesus when he decided to punish his offender. In this version, the reason behind the curse is to force the Jew not to travel but to flee. The Jew must leave his home because of a pogrom, because he is hungry, because he is jobless. He has to escape from the threat of concentration camps, gulags, mercenaries, multinational oil companies, deforestation teams, drought and flooding, military or religious dictatorships. He must cross vast deserts and great mountains, he must venture onto the sea with Christ's cross on his shoulders, and under the lash of the police and the jeering of the crowd. He must force himself to imagine that on the other side he will find generous people who will welcome him, allow him to lead a decent life, freed of a fault that was never truly his. He must wait, in a refugee center in northern France or southern Italy, or in the desperate caravans fleeing the violence of Central America or Syria, for the arrival of the promised redeemer, while in the far distance he tries to make out the longed-for trumpets of Judgment Day.

SLEEPING BEAUTY

Hers is a story about time: time lost, time delayed, time of waiting, of dreaming, of inexperience. It gets off to a bad start. At her birth the Sleeping Beauty is blessed by the fairies, all except one, whom the king forgot to invite and who therefore casts a spell on the child that she will die from the prick of a poisoned spindle. Neither royal decrees nor the magic of the good fairies can dispel the power of spite: forbidding all spindles and changing

the sleep of death into a never-ending dream will not alter the awful curse. While the adults seek inefficient solutions, the child becomes a woman, touches a spindle, and sinks into a deep slumber. At that same moment, the entire castle falls asleep, in expectation of the true love's kiss that will one day (they hope) awaken them all. Around the Sleeping Princess, time stops.

Several writers have copied Beauty's method with a similar narrative intent: to preserve the world as it once was, frozen but still alive, in a dusty castle or a buried Pompeii. This is what takes place in Rip Van Winkle's story told by Washington Irving, in the monastery of Shangri-La described by James Hilton in *Lost Horizon,* in Adolfo Bioy Casares's *The Perjury of the Snow,* in Wagner's *Ring* cycle when Wotan puts Brünnhilde to sleep, in Agatha Christie's *At Bertram's Hotel.* Romania under Nicolae Ceauşescu, Spain in the sixties, the Tea Party states today perhaps found an unconscious inspiration in these literary examples in which being asleep can hardly be distinguished from being dead.

Beauty's sleep: Is this what makes her attractive to the Prince? That she lies motionless and silent, her eyes closed, unable to resist or react? The young Pablo Neruda, in one of his twenty love poems, put into simple verse this ancient male fantasy:

> I like it when you're silent because you seem as
> absent,
> You hear me from afar and my voice doesn't
> reach you,

As if your eyes had flown and were no longer
with me,
As if your mouth were sealed by the touch of a
kiss.

Edgar Allan Poe did not mince words. In *The Philosophy of Composition* he wrote that a beautiful dead woman was "unquestionably the most poetical topic in the world." You cannot get more silent than that.

Death and sleep have intermingled since literature's earliest afternoons. More than forty centuries ago, in the Epic of Gilgamesh, the poet called sleep the brother of death, and this terrible or consoling notion has kept its dark prestige ever since. In the sleep of death time stops, as Saint Anselm tells us is the custom of Paradise; in the sleep of earthly nights, time flows on, but the dreamers are condemned to wait for the moment allotted for their waking up. In the *Siete Partidas* of Alfonso the Wise the story is told of a monk who wished to know what time in Paradise was like. One morning he heard a bird sing outside his window. He went into the garden the better to hear the song, and a voice whispered in his ear: "This is a mere second of celestial time." Overjoyed, he returned to his cell and found that his brother monks had died long since and that in the brief moment it took for the bird to sing, three hundred centuries had gone by. Time in paradise (theologians say) has no duration because every instant offers everything there is to have. In hell, however, time lasts eternally because nothing ever takes place there: without hope nothing can happen except a hopeless waiting. Carl Gustav Jung recalled that an uncle of his once stopped him on the street and asked, "Do you know how God torments the sinners?" Jung shook his head. "He makes them wait," the uncle answered, and went on his way.

Beauty's sleep: does it take place in paradise or in hell? In her castle, time does not go by, which makes us think the former; her sleep, however, is an endless waiting, which suggests the latter. If it takes place in paradise, her awakening will never occur, since there, waking up would imply the interruption of a constant present, a blessed status quo in which the Princess keeps on being beautiful, endlessly innocent, endlessly longed-for by princes dressed in blue. But if her sleep is an infernal one, then Beauty slumbers in the moment just before her innocence comes to an end, because if a Prince were to arrive and wake her, he would condemn Beauty to the yoke of Time, forcing her to retrieve in one single instant the passing of the years in the world outside. Beauty would wake up but her skin would suddenly wrinkle, her sight would become dim, her pearl-white teeth would fall out, her golden hair would turn gray, and her terrified Prince would be of the age of a possible grandson, if not great-grandson. In this case, there is no happy end either.

That was perhaps the true curse of the fairy whom the king forgot: not to grow old gracefully, not to advance gradually in knowledge and experience, not to enjoy the turning of the wheel of the seasons. To be condemned (if she wants to be the woman the Prince saw asleep) to plastic surgeries, to Botox, to breast implants, to injections of monkey-gland serum.

She has, however, another option. She can reject the curse, reject the blessings, reject the sleeping courtiers, reject her parents' breach of etiquette, reject the Constant Prince. And imitating Ibsen's Nora and Carmen Laforet's Andrea (two of Beauty's latter-day children), she can slam the door of the Enchanted Castle and face the world with eyes wide open.

PHOEBE

Of the four Caulfield siblings in *The Catcher in the Rye*
Phoebe is the youngest. She is the most intelligent, the
most empathetic, the least selfish, the most intuitive. Allie,
the brother who preceded her, never got mad at anyone
and died very young of leukemia. Holden came next, and
the eldest, D.B., left for Hollywood, where he drives a
Jaguar and (according to Holden) prostitutes his writing
talent. The Caulfields are a literary family: before selling
himself to Hollywood, D.B. published a "terrific" book

of stories called *The Secret Goldfish*. Allie wrote poems in green ink all over the fingers and pocket of his baseball mitt "so that he'd have something to read when he was in the field and nobody was up at bat." Holden himself is a reader and looks to the books he likes for the logic that is absent in the world. His list of favorite authors is impressive: it includes Dickens, Isak Dinesen, Ring Lardner, Somerset Maugham (with some caveats), Thomas Hardy, Shakespeare, Rupert Brooke, Emily Dickinson, F. Scott Fitzgerald, and Hemingway. And Phoebe writes books about a girl detective called Hazle (*sic*) Weatherfield. Typically, Phoebe never finishes these books.

Phoebe, according to Holden, is "very emotional, for a child." But "you'd like her," he assures us. "I mean if you tell old Phoebe something, she knows exactly what the hell you're talking about. I mean you can even take her anywhere with you. If you take her to a lousy movie, for instance, she knows it's a lousy movie. If you take her to a pretty good movie, she knows it's a pretty good movie."

Phoebe is red-haired, like their brother Allie was, and wears her hair very short in the summertime, sticking it behind her pretty ears. "In the wintertime," Holden explains, "it's pretty long, though. Sometimes my mother braids it and sometimes she doesn't. It's really nice, though. She's only ten. She's quite skinny, like me, but nice skinny." We don't know if Holden has come across the lines in the Song of Songs: "We have a little sister, and she hath no breasts: what shall we do for our sister in the day when she shall be spoken for?" Holden does not think that far.

When D.B. is away in Hollywood, skinny Phoebe occupies his room with its oversize bed and oversize desk, "to spread out." She keeps the broken bits of the record Holden has bought for her (and then accidentally dropped) because she likes to put order in the world, and is upset by Holden's inability to do the same. She is thrifty: she can help Holden materially by giving him the money she has saved for Christmas: "Eight dollars and eighty-five cents. *Sixty*-five cents. I spent some," she explains.

Above all, Phoebe can pinpoint exactly the root of Holden's existential angst. "You don't like *any*thing that's happening," she tells him, because as she rightly sees, Holden seems unable to find enjoyment in anything. Dante would have placed Holden in the circle of the wrathful who "are sullen in the sweet air that is made happy by the sun." Phoebe, however, enjoys the world and its challenges, and is brave and up for anything, so when Holden tells her he is leaving to go out West, she packs her bag and wants to go with him. Without Holden being aware of or understanding it, she serves as his eyes, watching out for the dangers in the road ahead. Stout-heartedly, she wants to be by his side when he encounters them.

Sometime in the mid-fifth century B.C.E., Euripides wrote a play about Antigone, of which only a few fragments have come down to us. Antigone, whose loving hand has washed the body of her brother Polynices clean and poured the ritual wine, is determined to have his remains buried properly, much against the king's orders. "But I will bury him," she says in one of the surviving verses, "and if I must die, I say that this crime is holy: I shall lie down with him in death, and I shall be as dear to him as he is to me." Holden tries to imagine what

Phoebe would feel if he got pneumonia and died. Phoebe would probably feel much the way Antigone does.

But where does all Phoebe's love and devotion, all her awareness and steadfastness, all her courage and intelligence, leave her? Her ancestral mirror is perhaps the young sister in the Grimms' story of the Six Swans. Six brothers have been turned into swans by witchcraft and can only be freed if their young sister weaves six shirts for them out of nettles gathered with her bare hands, and does not utter a word for six full years. When the six years are almost over, she is discovered by a prince who instantly falls in love with her and wants to marry her, but because she will not say a single word, his courtiers convince him that she is a witch and must be burned. On the eve of the execution, in her cell with her bundle of nettles, she manages to finish the last of the shirts except for one sleeve and throws them over the six swans. The brothers recover their human form (the youngest keeps one feathery wing) and explain to the prince the brave reason for their sister's silence.

In that story, all ends well, but will all end well for Phoebe? On the last page of the book, watching his sister as she sits on the carousel horse while the rain falls down in buckets, Holden feels happy, almost for the first time. "I don't know why," he says. "It was just that she looked so damn *nice,* the way she kept going around and around, in her blue coat and all."

Like the stories about Hazle Weatherfield that Phoebe never finishes, Phoebe shines brightly throughout the novel, circling around her blurry-eyed brothers but never following an orbit of her own, never reaching her own conclusion. Mourning a brother she knows she'll never see again, taking up the room of the prodigal firstborn in the family home, protecting and guiding Holden in his spellbound state, and even correcting his pipe dream of catching kids in a field of rye at the edge of a cliff ("It's 'If a body *meet* a body coming through the rye,'" she tells him), Phoebe simply keeps on going "around and around, in her blue coat and all" to the tune of "Smoke Gets in Your Eyes."

HSING·CHEN

Three are the tasks usually assigned to the heroine or hero in fairy tales; the birds who search for their king in Attar's *Conference of the Birds* have to cross seven valleys or seven seas of which the one before the last is called Vertigo and the last Annihilation; the plagues which the Egyptian Pharaoh endures before freeing the Israelites are ten; also ten are the terraces that cleanse the saved sinners in Dante's Purgatory, if we include the two preliminary terraces and the crowning Garden of Eden; the labors of

Hercules are twelve. The trials endured in any human undertaking vary in number and intensity.

Eight are the stages required for the redemption of the fallen Buddhist monk Hsing-chen in the seventeenth-century Korean classic *The Nine Cloud Dream,* attributed by most historians to the eminent scholar Kim Man-jung. Each of these eight corresponds to a certain beautiful fairy maiden to whom he not unwillingly makes love, and whose names sound, to jaded Western ears, like echoes of those of country-western stars: Rainbow Phoenix, Moonlight, Shy Wild Goose, Jasper Shell Blossom, Spring Cloud, Panpipe Harmony Orchid, Cloud of Starlings, Whitecap.

Hsing-chen (his name means "Original True Nature" or "Carnal Desire") is punished for breaking the laws of his Buddhist master, Liu-kuan, lord of Lotus Peak Monastery. After being tempted into drinking wine by the Dragon King, Hsing-chen, his mind befuddled, uses his mystical powers to turn blossoms into jewels to please the eight fairy ladies. For this sin, he is condemned to the curious fate of reincarnating as the most heroic of men and undergoing a sort of carnal *Pilgrim's Progress.* Under the name Shao-yu (Small Visitor) he is reborn into a poor peasant family and thereafter brought up by his widowed mother. Once he reaches manhood, Shao-yu successfully passes the court examinations and enters the Emperor's service as the Imperial Archivist. Later he acquires the skills of a poet, a musician, a diplomat, and a soldier, and rises in society to become the brother-in-law of the Emperor himself.

Set in ninth-century Tang China, in the golden age of

Chinese cosmopolitan culture, *The Nine Cloud Dream* is a magical bildungsroman, the chronicle of an education in Confucian, Daoist, and Buddhist truths. "Meetings and farewells, farewells and meetings—that is the way of the world," is how a Buddhist sage sums up Shao-yu's learning journey through life. Eventually, Shao-yu succeeds both in defeating an invading Tibetan army by arranging his troops according to the *I Ching,* and bedding the eight maidens to whom he has been destined, even (as in the case of the seventh maiden) in the midst of a terrible battle, with the gleam of the sword serving as a nuptial candle and the boom of the army gongs replacing the sound of lutes. After so many successes, Shao-yu suddenly finds himself confronted by an elderly monk who reveals himself to be his old master and tells him that everything that has taken place in his life as a mortal was nothing but a fleeting dream, an entire lifetime of love and war experienced in a single moment of deep meditation. With this revelation, Shao-yu (restored to the person of Hsing-chen) achieves enlightenment and thereafter dedicates himself to teaching the perfect doctrine of the Right Way. Eventually he becomes the lord of the Lotus Peak Monastery, and immortals and dragons, men and spirits alike revere him as they had in the past revered his master. The eight maidens too abandon their worldly ways and seek enlightenment, becoming true bodhisattvas, devoted souls entitled to Nirvana but compassionately delaying the moment in order to save other mortals from suffering. At long last, as had been decreed from the start, Hsing-chen and the fairy ladies enter hand in hand the groves of the Buddhist paradise.

Many times throughout the amorous adventures we are given clues to the dreamlike quality of what we think is the real world. "The eye perceives more truth than two ears," someone says to Shao-yu shortly before he is deceived by a beautiful girl who tells him she is a ghost but is later revealed to be real. It doesn't matter in what direction the trickery is effected: as a girl who is a ghost or as a ghost who is a real girl. "Men and ghosts have different paths," the woman explains to Shao-yu later, "but love can bring them together." What matters in the end is knowing that the world of the senses is unreal and the world of the spirit is the true one; the former is merely a fantasy, the latter is the only reality that counts.

How astonishing that dreamed-up creatures are the ones who tell us that our life is a dream. Segismundo in Calderón's *Life Is a Dream* complains that in our singular world living is but dreaming and that experience teaches that whoever lives dreams what he is until he awakes. Prospero in *The Tempest* explains that we are such stuff as dreams are made on and our little life is rounded with a sleep. Tweedledee and Tweedledum say to Alice that she is only a sort of thing in the Red King's dream and if he were to wake, she would "go out—bang!—just like a candle!"

Several months after his shipwreck, Hsing-chen's contemporary, the Yorkshire mariner Robinson Crusoe, all alone on his island, has a terrible dream. He sees himself sitting on the ground outside the wall of his enclosure and suddenly observes a man descending from a great black cloud in a bright flame of fire. No sooner has the man landed than he moves forward towards the dreamer, a long spear in his hand, seemingly ready to kill him. With a dreadful voice, the man says to Crusoe, "Seeing that all these things have not brought thee to repentance, now thou shalt die." Crusoe finds it impossible to describe the impression that remained in his mind when he woke up and found that the vision was nothing but a dream. For Crusoe, the hardships of his solitary island life are the awful reality, and the dream merely a warning. For Hsing-chen it is the crowded life of love and action that reveals itself to be the cautionary dream.

If Hsing-chen (in the skin of Shao-yu) has to complete his earthly journey through feats of war and love-making, and if all these accomplishments, military and amorous, amount to nothing but the shadow of a shadow, what are we, his readers, shadows following the shadow of a shadow on the page? In the fable that Plato has Socrates tell in the *Republic,* perceived reality is but the shadow of the world reflected on the wall of the cave we live in, and Socrates (and Plato himself) also look upon these cast shadows and take them to be real. For the men and women of seventeenth-century Korea, ninth-century China (in which Hsing-chen's adventures are set) was a vast and ever-present shadow, both threatening and alluring, like a multifaceted and tumultuous troubling dream from which they one day hoped to wake.

"Who can say, then, what really exists and what does not?" Shao-yu reflects towards the end of his story. "The Buddha said a man's body is a transitory illusion, like foam on the water or flower petals in a gust of wind."

JIM

He belongs to what Tennessee Williams called "the fugitive kind," together with Jean Valjean in *Les Misérables,* the gaucho Martín Fierro, who deserted from the army in the eponymous Argentinian epic, Frankenstein's Monster escaping into the frozen North, the convict Abel Magwitch in *Great Expectations.* He is defined not by who he is as he knows himself to be but by an imposed state of fugue, forced by the outside world to light out "mighty quick." But how? "You see," he explains to Huckleberry

Finn, "ef I kep' on tryin' to git away afoot de dogs 'ud track me; ef I stole a skift to cross over, dey'd miss dat skift you see, en dey'd know 'bout whah I'd lan' on de yuther side en whah to pick up my track." Trapped between the ever-present prejudices of the adult whites and the irresponsible games of the adolescent whites, Jim tries to walk away to some utopian place of equal rights: a Free State in Mark Twain's novel, the Underground Railroad to Canada in American history, the land of the low-swinging sweet chariot in the black gospel imagination. Like his other fugitive comrades, Jim will never reach it. He will be recognized as a freed slave but not as himself, as whatever that magically conjured-up being might be for him.

The white world has plans for Jim: Aunt Polly and Uncle Silas and Aunt Sally want to make "a heap of fuss over him" to reward him for some "good deed" and give him "all he wanted to eat, and a good time, and nothing to do," much as they would treat a faithful pet. Tom Sawyer (his ill-fated scheme inspired by the adventure stories he has read) imagines that he and Huck, after they have succeeded in their plan, will take Jim "back up home on a steamboat, in style, and pay him for his lost time, and write word ahead and get out all the niggers around, and have them waltz him into town with a torchlight procession and a brass band"—a cross between the entry of Christ into Jerusalem and the freak performance of a dancing bear. *Don Quixote* (one of the books that Tom Sawyer has read) could have inspired the boy to fight against injustice; instead he finds in the knight's bookish madness merely the thrill of pirate adventures and the power of fairy-tale enchantments. Maybe if Jim had come across *Don Quixote,* his reading might have been a different one from Tom's.

But slaves were not taught to read. In 1660, King Charles II had proclaimed his loyalty to the Protestant faith according to which, as Luther had taught, the salvation of the soul depended on each individual's ability to read the word of God for him- or herself. Accordingly, the king decreed that the Council for Foreign Plantations should instruct natives, household servants, and slaves in the precepts of Christianity. But the slave owners were not convinced. They feared that a slave who learned to read the Bible might also read abolitionist tracts and even find in Scripture stories such as that of Moses and Pharaoh excuses to revolt. The royal decree was strongly opposed in the American colonies, and strongest of all in South Carolina, where, barely a century later, strict laws were issued that forbade all blacks, whether free or slaves, to be taught to read. These laws were still in effect in Mark Twain's day. A slave who infringed the law for the first time was whipped with a cowhide, the second with a cat-o-nine-tails, and the third had the first joint of the forefinger cut off. In several cases, slaves who became literate and taught others to read were hanged.

Jim, of course, cannot read. Had he learned, as Frederick Douglass explains in his autobiography, with a resolution born of his master's determination "to keep me in ignorance," he might have come across Aristotle's justification for slavery. "For that some should rule and others be ruled is a thing not only necessary, but expedient," argued that order-obsessed philosopher in his *Politics.*

"From the hour of their birth, some are marked out for subjection, others for rule. . . . And indeed the use made of slaves and of tame animals is not very different; for with their bodies both minister to the needs of life." Aristotle felt that it was not necessary to explain that by "needs" he meant the needs of himself and his kind.

Thomas Aquinas, in his vast *Summa Theologica,* equated the relationship of a master and his slave with that of a father and his son, and argued that both the son and the slave should enjoy certain rights. "A son, as such, belongs to his father, and a slave, as such, belongs to his master; yet each, considered as a man, is something having a separate existence and is distinct from others. Hence in so far as each of them is a man, there is justice towards them of a certain kind, and for this reason too there are certain laws regulating the bonds between a father and his son, and between a master and his slave. But in so far as each is something belonging to another, the perfect idea of 'right' or 'just' is wanting in their case." This, as Aquinas certainly knew, is a facile syllogism in which the conclusion is implied in the premise, because a possession, slave or child or dog, cannot by definition claim the rights or the justice claimed by its owner. Huck's Pop agrees with Aquinas. A father who has raised a son should expect that the son should "do suthin' for him" and a white man who is a decent citizen should have more rights than "a prowling, thieving, infernal, white-shirted free nigger."

Since Aristotle, and even earlier, every society that has accepted the concept of slavery as a just one has defended it on these two presumptions: that it is right for those considered (by themselves) superior to have absolute power over those considered inferior and that the condition of slavery is often agreeable to those enslaved. "This is for your own good" and "This hurts me more than it does you" are the two aberrant phrases of parents who believe in "spare the rod and spoil the child."

In the preface to the sado-masochistic classic *Story of O,* the man-of-letters Jean Paulhan, under the title "The Pleasures of Slavery," tells the story of the freeing of slaves in Barbados in 1838. Some two hundred men and women who were granted their freedom returned to their old master, a certain Mr. Glenelg, and begged him to take them back. Glenelg, perhaps out of respect for the anti-slavery laws, refused. The former slaves protested with increasing violence and then proceeded to massacre Glenelg and his entire family. After that, says Paulhan, they returned to their huts and took up their customary labors. If the story is true, it must have elicited many an "I told you so" among the remaining slave owners of the American South.

But unlike those Barbados slaves, Jim is not content with his condition, and if he were able to reach a free port, he would certainly not ask to come back. We are told of Jim's morals (as when he pours scorn on Solomon's judgment and expresses pity for the imprisoned son of Louis XVI), of his beliefs (in the power of magic and the obligation to respect the dead, and in the truth told in dreams), of his determination to be free and become his own person by rights, and reclaim his family ("when he got to a free State he would go to saving up money and never spend a single cent, and when he got enough he would buy his wife, which was owned on a farm close to where Miss Watson lived; and then they would both work to buy the two children, and if their master wouldn't sell them, they'd get an Ab'litionist to go and steal them").

When I first read *Huckleberry Finn* at about the same age as Huck was, what moved me most was the growing relationship between Huck and Jim. In Jim, Huck had found (I thought) a father of sorts, an inverted mirror of Huck's abusive and bigoted Pop, a Pop who needed Huck in order to survive in the big, bad world, an Oedipus to Huck's Antigone. I envied Huck because I knew he needed Jim as much as Jim needed Huck.

In spite of clues scattered throughout the novel, in spite of the glimpses we are given of his character, Jim is still read merely in terms of his condition as a slave. Toni Morrison judged the portrayal of Jim as "an ill-made clown suit that cannot hide the man within" and saw in the novel's ending an effort on the part of Mark Twain to accommodate "a racist readership" by making Jim "so complete a buffoon." In Sophocles' *Oedipus Rex,* the seer Tiresias calls Oedipus a "poor fool."

That racist readership that Morrison identifies is still the novel's readership today because, in the United States certainly, racism colors everything. The verb is abominably apt. Whether the establishment of a social hierarchy in black and white allowed for slavery, or whether slavery required a justification that society invented as a hierarchy of white and black is a question that can be endlessly debated.

But where does all this leave Jim?

Slavery was practiced in the New World from the

early days of the colonial governments; at the time of the American Declaration of Independence in 1776 it was still legal in all thirteen colonies. Slavery was not abolished nationally until almost a century later, in 1865, when the Thirteenth Amendment freed the last forty thousand slaves in the two remaining slave states of Kentucky and Delaware. A few decades earlier, Alexis de Tocqueville had observed that in the United States a multiracial society without slavery was, in his opinion, untenable; he was convinced that the deep-rooted prejudice against black people would increase were they to be granted further rights. In other words, don't look for the cause; temper the treatment, and you won't exacerbate the symptoms.

This attitude still runs today just below the surface in the United States. As soon as the authorities appear to water down the discourse against prejudice, Pop's words gush back into the public forum. In 2018, complaints to the Equal Employment Opportunity Commission increased by 17 percent from the previous year and, according to FBI statistics, hate crimes in 2017 increased by almost one thousand cases; just under 50 percent of all hate crimes in the United States are committed against blacks. One in every sixty-five black men murdered in the United States is killed by the police; roughly 25 percent of these victims were unarmed. Jim is still on the run.

Forbes magazine announced that in 2018, the United States was the country with the largest number of billionaires in the world, most of them leading, we presume, happy lives. Forty-five years earlier, in 1973, Ursula K. Le Guin published a short story called "The Ones Who Walk

Away from Omelas." Omelas is a town where everyone enjoys a perfectly happy life. The one condition for this communal happiness is that once a year, during the summer festival, every citizen has to file past a narrow room in the basement of one of the loveliest town buildings, where a naked child (Le Guin does not specify either the sex or the color of its skin) is kept locked up, sitting in its own filth. The child has not always lived in that room and can remember sunlight and its mother's voice. "I will be good," it says. "Please let me out. I will be good!"

Le Guin adds that at times, someone will go to see the child and will not go home content. Sometimes someone will go out into the street and keep walking, and walk straight out of the city of Omelas. Le Guin says she does not know where these people are headed, but she knows that there are some who walk away from Omelas.

THE CHIMERA

The Royal Tyrrell Museum in Alberta, Canada, is justly famous for its dinosaur collection. But perhaps its strangest exhibit is not of the colossal skeletons of beasts that roamed when humans were not around to see them but a display showing enlarged forms of microscopic marine animals that were not destined to survive for more than a very brief moment in the vast time of prehistory, three hundred million years ago. Floating in a gloomy sea of Plexiglas, their transparent bodies outlined

in white, luminous shapes many times larger than their actual size, these failed sketches of living things seem to the untrained eye nightmarishly askew and asymmetrical, half-hearted efforts to depict creatures that might have been, as if an artist had doodled shapes with closed eyes and then, realizing what had been done, erased them forever. These never fully accomplished phantoms are among the most terrifying monsters ever seen, compared to which Medusa and the basilisk are tame, almost mundane. Life on our planet begins with monsters, not with the common species to which we are accustomed.

The word *monster* derives from the Latin verb *monere*, "to warn." The monster is the prodigy, the freak, the unusual being, the thing unexpected, that which is seldom or never seen. Horace, to refer to something monstrously impossible, speaks of black swans, not knowing that at that very moment (as Borges pointed out) flocks of black swans were darkening the skies of Australia. There is always the possibility, however small, that what we call an impossible monster is lurking right now in an obscure corner of the universe.

Because we lack the ingenuity of nature that, Dante tells us, "does not repent of her elephants and whales," our imaginary monsters are bigger or smaller versions of what nature has already conceived, or mere combinations of bits and pieces of what can be seen in any zoo. Fish, bird, or lion paired with a woman; horse, bull, or lizard paired with a man; stallions and serpents that can fly; theological inventions with many arms like Shiva or a triple personality like the Holy Trinity; dragons with a thousand heads or people with none: our imaginary bestiaries are little more than ostentatious versions of a *cadavre exquis,* the game invented by the surrealists that consists of drawing, on a piece of paper folded over many times, a section of a body without seeing the efforts of the previous players. The results are often absurd or funny, but rarely as astonishing as a giraffe or a platypus. As God says to Job with a touch of the braggart: "Gavest thou the goodly wings unto the peacocks? or wings and feathers unto the ostrich?"

So ingrained is our belief in monsters that Christopher Columbus, observing three manatees close to the mouth of the Orinoco, stated in his journal that he saw three mermaids swimming in the sea, but added with scrupulous precision that "they are not as beautiful as they are reported to be." Our monsters exist because we want them to exist, perhaps because we need them to exist.

The Chimera is the archetypal composite monster. Homer described the Chimera as "a thing of immortal make, not human / lion-fronted and snake behind, a goat in the middle / and snorting out the breath of the terrible flame of bright fire." Hesiod makes her (because the Chimera is female) the daughter of another monster, the viper-woman Echidna, and says that the fearful Chimera is huge, swift-footed, and strong, with three heads like the dog Cerberus, who guards the entrance to the Underworld: "one head is that of a lion, the other of a dragon, the third of a goat." Other poets wrote that the Chimera gave birth to the Sphinx (defeated by Oedipus) and the Nemean lion (killed by Hercules). The Chimera herself was vanquished by the hero Bellerophon mounted on the winged horse Pegasus. Monsters in our imagination seem always to come to a bad end.

And yet, a few of the monsters imagined by our ancestors are resilient enough to have persisted throughout time. Unlike the Chimera, the centaur and the mermaid, the dragon and the griffin, the ogre and the satyr still roam our world. The Chimera, instead, is less a creature than a symbol. According to Robert Graves, the Chimera was for the Greeks a calendar emblem of the Trinitarian year "of which the seasonal emblems were lion, goat, and serpent." For us in our time, the Chimera is the representation of the impossible, a name we give to that which can be imagined but never achieved, like a life without pain or a just society for all.

Who are our monsters today? Those whom we cannot bear to include in the human fold, those against whom we are warned because of their "inhuman" acts. Hitler, Stalin, Pinochet, Bashar al-Assad, serial killers, and rapists have all been called monsters because they have done things that we would like to imagine no human being could possibly do. The ancients were wiser. Their gods and their monsters had supernatural qualities and defects but they had common human defects and qualities as well: Polyphemus was a dupe, Cerberus was greedy, the centaurs were wise, the Dragon-lady of Lusignan seductive, Pegasus boasted of his speed and the Hydra of her strength. These monsters are memorable because, like us humans, they can feel pride and hate and lust—and envy and weariness too—because, beyond our fear, they elicit respect as fellow creatures of this earth, desiring kindness as we do and enduring suffering as we do. Jean Cocteau suggested that the Sphinx met her end because she herself whispered the answer of the riddle to Oedipus, with whom she had fallen in love.

Unlike the age of our forebears, ours is both credulous and skeptical. We profess to be rationalists and scientific minded, yet we believe in little green men from outer space (the Saint Lawrence Insurance Company of Altamonte, in Florida, offers a policy against alien abduction), in the Abominable Snowman and the Loch Ness Monster (tours are organized for possible sightings), in vampires (as recently as February 2004, in Romania, several members of a certain Petre family feared that one their deceased relatives had become a vampire; they dug up his corpse, tore out his heart, burned it, mixed the ashes with water and drank it). The ancients socialized their monsters but also felt responsible for their existence: the Minotaur was born because of the lust of Pasiphaë, and the Mermaids came to life to prevent mariners from going beyond the forbidden limits. As the historian Paul Veyne explained, "Of course the ancients believed in their myths!" But did they think them true? "Truth," answers Veyne, "is the thin layer of gregarious self-satisfaction that separates us from the will to power."

Today we believe in monsters but we do not want to feel responsible for them. For us, the existence of a monster such as the Chimera is no longer a question of truth but of evading the truth, of refusing to admit that we are capable, each and every one of us, of the most admirable deeds and the most abominable crimes.

ROBINSON CRUSOE

We never land on a desert island without longing to leave it. Anchored on the mainland, we dream of sailing beyond the horizon and arriving on a savage shore where we can build a world however we see fit, where we can become the despotic ruler of a tiny private universe. But once on the island, once suffering from cold, hunger, fear, boredom, and despair, all we can think of is a way of getting off. When G. K. Chesterton was asked what book

he would take to a desert island, he answered, "Thomas'
Guide to Practical Shipbuilding."

It should not surprise us then that it was the inhabitants of an island who populated the sea with nonexistent
islands, inventing for them marvelous geographies and
thrilling stories. A continental people hardly requires the
re-creation of other lands: beyond those mountains, those
woods, or those valleys, there live surely other people
who are their reflection and whose stories echo their
own. On an island, however, there are no "other lands":
everything is immediately perceivable, nothing is hidden
away. That is why the Anglo-Saxons, in order to conjure
up other manners of being, invented unseen islands that
lay always just beyond the horizon, islands that might or
might not be one day discovered but that required no
physical presence in order to exist. That imaginary cartography has a prehistory in Greece, in China, and in
the Arab world, but the three fundamental categories to
which, without exception, every imaginary island belongs
were dreamt up and defined over barely two short centuries by the islanders of Great Britain: Thomas More's
Utopia, the insular kingdoms visited by Captain Lemuel
Gulliver, and the island of Robinson Crusoe.

On April 25, 1719, there appeared in London two
octavo volumes bearing the title *The Life and Strange
Surprizing Adventures of Robinson Crusoe of York, Mariner,*
purporting to be a true account "Written by Himself."
It was an immediate success. According to the secret
author, Daniel Defoe, this was not fiction: he was inventing truthful chronicles in the tradition of the historians

whom Herodotus repudiated. It mattered little that the book was not the reliable testimony it claimed to be: the immediacy of the harrowing narrative was enough to persuade the readers of its accuracy. The narrator might be fictitious, Defoe's readers argued, but the events recounted were true.

So they were. Some fifteen years before the book was published, in 1704, a sailor called Alexander Selkirk was marooned by his captain for reasons unknown on the uninhabited island of Juan Fernández, close to the Chilean coast, from where he was rescued five years later, in 1709. Selkirk's story inspired Defoe, who enlarged and improved on it, turning the sailor's account into the founding chronicle of a primitive society that, according to one of his prestigious and enthusiastic readers, Karl Marx, "illustrated economic theory in action." Crusoe is the *Homo primus,* an Adam who institutes all the human arts and skills. His island becomes the exemplary model for all human activities, and in its unique development shows the intrinsic possibilities of a workable society. He can philosophically imagine the possibilities of an entirely new world because (as the German scholar Hans Blumenberg has noted) "shipwreck, as seen by the survivor, is the figure of a primordial philosophical experience."

Although in the end Robinson Crusoe returns to his native soil, his readers know that he will never really abandon the island where he was lord of the world, master of his domain: anywhere else he is just another Englishman. Whatever Selkirk's wish, Robinson cannot be rescued. Borges, in his 1964 sonnet "Alexander Selkirk," gives these words to the original Crusoe, on his arrival in England:

> And I am no longer he who eternally
> Looked at the sea and its deep barren plain.
> But now what shall I do so it may find
> That I am here, and safe, among my kind?

As Crusoe's readers know, no one lands on a desert island for the first time. Even if we believe that no other has set foot on this particular stretch of sand, the act of arrival exists already in our literary memory. Since that morning of October 1659 when Crusoe arrived on the island, more or less hopefully, we have endlessly repeated his primordial gesture. The Swiss family Robinson, the eternally shipwrecked bunch of *Gilligan's Island,* the followers of Lord of the Flies, the pathetic contestants of reality TV, the enthusiastic Neil Armstrong on the island of the moon—all follow the choreography established by Daniel Defoe for his poor English gentleman. Because Crusoe is, of course, a gentleman. He speaks no other language than English (he tells us that he left on board the wreck several volumes belonging to the ship's captain because they were in Portuguese); his faith is that of the Church of England (he also leaves behind a few papist books); he firmly believes that all those who are not like him are savages (i.e., cannibals, i.e., black); and he confidently takes on the task of bringing civilization to the wild world beyond the borders of the empire (even if that world is little more than a clump of windswept rocks). He knows how to do everything: build a house, erect a fence, draw maps of the virgin territory, tan a goat's hide, sew himself a suit, plant wheat, bake clay pots, cook. So many tasks accomplished in the name of the British crown, and no one to admire his labors!

So Defoe brings in Crusoe's Man Friday. Without Friday, without the primitive, uncivilized Friday, Crusoe's deeds would remain sadly secret, lacking a fitting audience. Without his shadow (because, after all, what is Friday but a somber, rustic Crusoe, as lonely and as unhappy as the English one?), Crusoe would vanish. He would turn, like his Greek predecessor who drifted from island to island until he was allowed to return home, into a Nobody. Not even Nobody, because before Friday appears in the story Crusoe is nameless, for he lacks a questioner—that is to say, a dialogue partner; that is to say, the possibility of active language; that is to say, of fruitful thought. The notebook in which Crusoe jots down his observations is not enough to lend him an identity: a writer needs a reader to bring the words to life since, as we know, literature is a binary art. Neither the dog, the cat, the goat, nor the parrot that appear one after the other in the castaway's life are enough: they are companionable animals but not conversing partners, merely a dummy audience for his monologues. Friday, instead, has a gift for languages, and with greater talent than Crusoe's, he will learn the tongue of Shakespeare in which Crusoe teaches him the tenets of Christian religion. Crusoe, however, will not learn Friday's language and therefore will never know of the wonderful system of beliefs Friday might have revealed to him. In short: Friday's presence is required for Crusoe to exist. In 1819, in his collection *West-östlicher Divan,* Goethe published a poem about the prehistoric ginkgo

biloba leaf that seems to have only one side but in effect
is double-sided:

> This small leaf that traveled eastward
> And now in my garden lies,
> offers rich and secret meanings
> That bear wisdom to the wise.
>
> Is it one green living creature
> Split in two and yet left whole?
> Are they two that fused together
> To become a single soul?
>
> The right answer to these questions
> Can be found by everyone.
> Can't you tell from my own verses
> That I'm also two and one?

Friday has existed in Crusoe's imagination since before
he left the docks of Hull. Long before he discovers Friday's
footstep in the sand, the savage is already in Crusoe's mind
as someone whose destiny, because he is not English,
Christian, or white, is to serve the gentleman who is all
these admirable things. For Friday, for the descendants of
Friday, the Declaration of the Rights of Man proclaimed
a century later will have no meaning whatsoever. Slavery
will be abolished, yes, but it will be merely replaced by
other forms of servitude: child labor, scant wages, land
expropriation, sex trade, genocide, destruction of natural
resources, industrially induced famine, displacements,
forced exile. Friday's destiny is then, if not to be a slave,
to be always something less than Crusoe. His role is to

be trained to serve in a field or a factory or an office or a sweatshop, to work for a master, to be humble and obsequious. Perhaps in order to teach this lesson in the arts of injustice, Rousseau chose *Robinson Crusoe* as the bedside book for his Émile.

QUEEQUEG

The only truly alien space is that of the body we inhabit. Everything else is open for exploration. The farthest stars and the deepest valleys of the ocean are open to human curiosity, but that which we call ours is only ours through an act of faith. We recognize our face in the mirror but we see it the wrong way round, left to right, and our back is as unknown to us as the far side of the moon (more so, because that hitherto secret area is now being carefully explored by the Chinese). Our adult

human skin covers an area of between sixteen and twenty-one square feet; of that surface, most of us can observe barely a third. John Donne, in his "Hymn to God, My God, in My Sickness," remarks that his "physicians by their love are grown / Cosmographers, and I their map." Our physicians can explore that map much more thoroughly than we can; it is as if we carried written on our skin a book that only others can read.

Some five centuries after Gutenberg invented the printing press, Kafka, in his story of the Penal Colony, imagined an infernal machine consisting of three parts: the lower one, on which the condemned prisoner is lain, is called the Bed, the upper one is the Inscriber, and the moving part in the middle is the Harrow. The Harrow carries two sorts of needles, long and short, arranged in rows. The long needle inscribes on the prisoner's skin the law that has been violated, the short one squirts water out to wash away the blood and keep the inscription clear. The whole contraption is an automatized writing machine, a monstrous parody of Gutenberg's invention, which, according to the historian Elizabeth Eisenstein, "made the words of God appear more multiform and His handiwork more uniform." The horror of Kafka's machine is that the condemned man does not know what the inscription is.

In *Moby-Dick,* the harpooner Queequeg carries on his skin hieroglyphic marks tattooed by a departed prophet and seer of his island of Kokovoko, marks that contain a complete theory of the heavens and the earth and a mystical treatise on the art of attaining truth. Queequeg, as Ishmael explains, was in his own person "a riddle to unfold; a wondrous work in one volume; but whose mysteries not even himself could read, though his own live heart beat against them." These mysteries "were therefore destined in the end to moulder away with the living parchment whereon they were inscribed, and so be unsolved to the last." This is what Ishmael thinks must have provoked Ahab to wildly exclaim one morning after surveying the tattooed man: "Oh, devilish tantalization of the gods!"

Ishmael also carries tattoos on his skin, but these are pages of a notebook on which he has inscribed facts and figures collected in his wild wanderings "because there was no other secure way to preserve information." On his right arm he has tattooed certain statistics about beached whales; the other parts of his body Ishmael has reserved "for a poem I was then composing." Queequeg's tattoos are the text of magical scribe, a universal text. Ishmael's are merely his own scribbles. When Ray Bradbury, who was later to write the script for John Huston's *Moby Dick,* dreamt up his Illustrated Man, he must have thought of Queequeg.

Queequeg cannot read. When he takes up a book, he counts the pages with deliberate regularity and at every fiftieth page he stops, looks vacantly around him, lets out an astonished whistle, and proceeds to the next fifty. Ishmael tries to explain to him the purpose of printing and the meaning of the book's illustrations, and this pedagogical act seems to create a bond between them as they lie in bed together, "a coy, loving pair": the man who can read but is uneasy with his life and seeks in sea voyages the equivalent of suicide, and the man who cannot read but is content with his own companionship and, like a true philosopher, is not unduly conscious of so living and so striving.

For Ishmael, the sea is a fiend to its own offspring, "worse than the Persian host who murdered his own guests," so unlike the "green, gentle, and most docile earth." Ishmael adjures the reader: "Consider them both, the sea and the land; and do you not find a strange analogy to something in yourself? For as this appalling ocean surrounds the verdant land, so in the soul of man lies one insular Tahiti, full of peace and joy, but encompassed by all the horrors of the half known life." And he warns the reader, and himself: "Push not off from that isle, thou canst never return!"

Queequeg is not worried by what he cannot know or cannot read. Signs exist, like the tattoos on his skin, and this is enough to make him happy and at peace with the world, a world that he judges "wicked in all meridians," and in which, obeying the charms of his little wooden god, Yojo, he has decided he'll "die a pagan."

Ishmael, however, is of the race of Stubb, the second mate, who believes that all visible objects are "as pasteboard masks" and that "in each event some unknown but still reasoning thing puts forth the mouldings for its features from behind the unreasoning mask." And he adds: "That inscrutable thing is what I chiefly hate." Queequeg seems not to know what hatred is.

When Queequeg falls ill and thinks he is dying, he refuses to be buried in a hammock and tossed like something vile to the death-devouring sharks. He wants to be buried in a coffin-canoe, and the carpenter on board makes him one out of "heathenish, coffin-coloured lumber" which had been cut from aboriginal groves in the Lackaday Islands. Queequeg places in the coffin his harpoon, a few ship's biscuits, a flask of fresh water, a small bag of woody earth, and a piece of sail-cloth rolled up for a pillow. Suddenly, without warning, Queequeg rallies: he recalls (like Socrates) an unpaid duty ashore and (unlike Socrates) he changes his mind about dying. Queequeg believes that, if a man makes up his mind to live, mere sickness cannot kill him: "nothing but a whale, or a gale, or some violent, ungovernable, unintelligent destroyer of that sort" can decree his end. Unused by Queequeg, the canoe-coffin will prove Ishmael's salvation at the end, as the ship is dragged down into the shrouding sea, when it shoots up like a life buoy and floats softly by his side. A day and a night later, Ishmael is rescued by the *Rachel,* searching for her missing children.

"Doubts of all things earthly, and intuitions of some things heavenly," says Ishmael, "this combination makes neither believer nor infidel, but makes a man who regards them both with equal eye." Queequeg is that man.

TYRANT BANDERAS

"Tyranny is not a matter of petty thefts and acts of violence, but of wholesale plunder, sacred and profane, private and public," says Socrates to his listeners in the ninth book of Plato's *Republic.* "And yet, the real tyrant is enslaved to cringing and to servitudes beyond compare, he is a flatterer of the basest of men, and so far from finding even the least satisfaction for his desires, he is in need of most things, and is truly a poor man, as is apparent to anyone who knows how to observe a soul.

Throughout his life he is filled with terror and suffers convulsions and pains; in fact he resembles the city he rules, and is its living image." And he concludes: "There is no city more wretched than that which is ruled by a tyrant."

Though Socrates' tyrant is a universal species, alive in every age and every country, Latin America seems to have been particularly propitious to his development, though the African continent in recent times and the Soviet bloc before the fall of the Wall are close contenders. Why one particular and vast chunk of the earth should display, over barely two centuries, such a catalogue of infamy, is perhaps an unanswerable question. In a letter written in 1830, the liberator Simón Bolívar foresaw this state of affairs, though he did not try to explain it. "America"—Bolívar gave Latin America the name of the entire continent—"is ungovernable for us. Those who serve the revolution plow the sea. The only thing to do in America is to emigrate. This land will infallibly fall into the hands of an unbridled crowd of petty tyrants almost too puny to notice and of all colors and races."

The fulfillment of Bolívar's prophecy allowed Carlos Fuentes, less than a century and half later, to suggest to his Latin American writer friends that they should each write a novel about their national tyrant and call the series "The Fathers of the Homeland." Fuentes realized that each of the twenty-seven countries of Latin America could boast (if that is the right word) of at least one tyrant; several had their pick of two or more. The project, unfortunately, never came to be realized, though it produced several masterpieces: in Colombia, Gabriel García Márquez's

The Autumn of the Patriarch; in Guatemala, Miguel Angel Asturias's *Señor Presidente;* in Paraguay, Augusto Roa Bastos's *I, the Supreme;* in Peru (though set in the Dominican Republic) Mario Vargas Llosa's *The Feast of the Goat.* Fuentes himself published in 1962 *The Death of Artemio Cruz.* To all the protagonists of these novels Socrates' definition can be applied.

The murky figure of the Latin American tyrant attracted as well writers from Europe. Beginning with Joseph Conrad's *Nostromo,* and continuing with Herbert Read's *The Green Child,* Graham Greene's *The Honorary Consul,* and, more recently, Daniel Pennac's *The Dictator and the Hammock,* European writers have recognized in the tyrants across the sea exotic versions of others closer to home. Among them, perhaps the most complex, the most puzzling is the protagonist of *Tyrant Banderas* by Ramón del Valle-Inclán.

Born in one of the poorest districts of rural Galicia in 1866, Valle-Inclán managed to enter the University of Santiago de Compostela and after graduating began work as a journalist in Madrid. Under the influence of the modernist poets (notably Rubén Darío, then living in Spain) his first publications were, as one critic called them, "lyrical effluvia," describing a world made for human enjoyment, subject to human will, in which the hero is the soldier-lover, a cross between Nietzsche's Superman and Tirso de Molina's Don Juan. It was perhaps during his 1916 journey to France as a war correspondent that Valle-Inclán radically changed his views on war and the uses of violence. From conservative aristocratic sympathies (he had presented himself as a right-wing candidate for the People's Chamber in 1910 and lost) the fifty-year-old writer switched his allegiance to the left (again he presented himself as a candidate, this time for the other side, and lost again). To depict the world as he now saw it, Valle-Inclán developed a harsh and unadorned prose in which he wrote his best-known plays and novels. He called these pieces *esperpentos,* that is to say, "grotesque and horrible things," the deformed reflection of classic motifs in European literature. The first of his *esperpento* novels (and the best) was *Tyrant Banderas.*

Tyrant Banderas is set in the imaginary South American country of Santa Fe de Tierra Firme, inspired by Valle-Inclán's experience of Mexico, which he visited first in 1892 as a thirty-four-year-old incipient writer and again in 1921 as a recognized author. After suffering censorship under the dictatorship of Primo de Rivera, who ruled Spain from 1923 to 1930 (Valle-Inclán was briefly imprisoned for his anti-Rivera opinions), he decided to transfer his depiction of Rivera's tyranny to the wilder Latin American landscapes he had known, in part to use elements of the dictatorship of Porfirio Díaz in Mexico, in part to feel free of documentary constraints. Not only Primo de Rivera and Porfirio Díaz served to inspire the character of Santos Banderas. In a letter to the scholar Alfonso Reyes, Valle-Inclán explained that *Tyrant Banderas* was "a novel about a tyrant with traits borrowed from Dr. Francia, Rosas, Melgarejo, López, Porfirio," all Latin American dictators. Whatever his sources, the experiment was immensely successful. "What I've written before *Tyrant Banderas* is fiddlesticks," Valle-Inclán confessed in an interview. "This novel is my first one. My work starts now." He was then sixty years old.

The biography of the man known as Santos Banderas, the Tyrant, is made up of fragments, snatches of dialogue, short scenes of action, but the patchwork effect is framed by a mathematically tight structure. Like Dante's *Commedia* (which Valle-Inclán read in his youth and greatly admired) the life of Banderas is built around the numbers three and seven: a prologue and an epilogue, then seven sections divided into books, seven books in the central section, three in each of the remaining six. The total number is twenty-seven (three times three times three). Furthermore, the story takes place over three days and is marked by three determining moments: the first in the prologue, the second halfway through the novel, the last in the third book of the third section.

This numerical insistence may be a reflection of Valle-Inclán's fascination with the occult, in which the numbers seven and three carry a particularly numinous charge. His main characters are believed to possess superhuman powers. Banderas himself is supposed, like Faust, to have signed a pact with the devil: he never sleeps, he has no intimate friends, he seems capable of the most incredible deeds. His opposer, Don Roque Cepeda, is also touched with a mysterious aura, but in his case his "occult" leanings come from his studies in theosophy, the ancient system of belief according to which the "seeker" was able to discover the working of all things visible and invisible, and communicate with ghosts. The entire atmosphere of the novel is imbued with a sense of the fantastic. Though nothing of this is made explicit, the uncanny, the otherworldly is constantly hinted at, in local superstitions, in the commentaries of the indigenous people, in the depiction of the landscape itself.

Banderas is almost pure *indio* with a few drops of Spanish blood. His is a violent and bloodthirsty temperament; he believes in rumors and encourages betrayal among his enemies, and yet he has a puritanical streak and professes to loathe adultery and prostitution. He is a taciturn man, stealthy in his movements, always dressed in black like a priest. He has a fierce, piercing look that can never be fully fathomed; his speech is ceremonious but deceitful; his laughter shrill and vinegary. Like many a Latin American tyrant (think of Rosas, Stroessner, Videla), Banderas considers himself a patriot, but the truth is that he merely delights in absolute power. Maybe this is the common link between tyrants in Latin America: they rise because of that "ungovernability" that Bolívar abominated, unchallenged by official constitutions and codes of law that seem, in many cases, nothing but rhetorical flourishes in a vast baroque pageant.

As suits this baroqueness, the tyrant's end is operatic, a sort of fulfilment of every one of his victims' unspoken dreams. Surrounded by his enemies in the Monastery of San Martín de los Monteses, Banderas knows he is doomed. His final act, to prevent his daughter from falling into the hands of his attackers, is to take a dagger and stab her himself, before falling dead under a shower of bullets. His head is cut off and exposed for three days in the plaza; the rest of his body is quartered and each section sent to one of the four main towns of Santa Fe de Tierra Firme.

Though the characters who surround Santos Banderas are themselves complex, many-faceted beings, it is the anonymous and swarming crowds around Banderas that are most powerfully alive. Soldiers, natives, prostitutes, servants, prisoners, peasants, diplomats, and politicians constitute an organic monster ever-present around the Tyrant. Our own experience in the twenty-first century confirms this: there is no tyrant who tweets or shouts his way to power without a fawning mass of unthinking and sacrificial supporters.

CIDE HAMETE BENEGELI

He is the greatest writer in the long history of Spanish literature. He wrote not in Castilian but in Aljamiado, a Romance language spoken by the converted Arabs of Spain. Like the Ladino spoken by Spanish Jews in their North African exile, Aljamiado is a mixture of Arabic and Castilian, a florid tongue that flourished in Arab Spain until it was brought to an abrupt close with the expulsion of the Moriscos in 1609. The novel for which he is famous could have been lost to us, as were lost those other great

books whose prestigious ghosts haunt our libraries: Homer's comic epic the *Margites,* which for Aristotle was "the parent of all comedies," or the second book of Aristotle's *Poetics,* which provides a motive for the murderer in Umberto Eco's *The Name of the Rose.* Thanks to a certain soldier with literary inclinations whose name was Miguel de Cervantes Saavedra, the masterpiece was saved.

We know that Cervantes (as he himself tells us) had begun to write the story of an elderly knight who lived in a Spanish town whose name he could not remember. Cervantes was at the time in prison, accused of a crime he claims he did not commit. Perhaps because of his unjust imprisonment, he began to imagine a man more ridiculous and braver than himself, a man determined, against all odds, to confront the everyday injustice of this world. Between four damp walls, "where all discomfort has its seat and all the sad noise of the world makes its home," no doubt reminiscent of an older and longer captivity on the north coast of Africa, the prisoner imagined a man who refuses to bend to the deceitful conventions of the world and who decides instead to obey nothing except the norms of his chosen ethics. To the hypocrisy of a society that demanded that citizens hide their own beliefs and live in appearances alone, his creation, Don Quixote, opposed to this the truth of absolute freedom, that of being able to choose his own ethical code and flaunt it in the face of those who will not admit it.

But then (this too Cervantes tells us), having reached the eighth chapter of the wondrous chronicle of his hero, inspiration fails him, and Cervantes stops the tale in the middle of a swashbuckling adventure. Unable to carry on, he finds himself one day strolling through the market-place of Toledo and sees in one of the stalls a tattered manuscript in Arabic script. Cervantes is one of those readers who reads everything, even torn bits of paper he finds in the street, and, curious to see what the manuscript might be about, he buys it and seeks a translator. He discovers one easily enough because, Toledo having long been one of the most prestigious centers of translation in Europe, in spite of the laws of expulsion it is common to find both Arabic and Hebrew translators in the market streets of the town. Cervantes then takes the translator to his house, and after a month and a half, and a payment of fifty pounds of raisins (translators' fees have not increased much since those ancient days), the rendering into Spanish of the adventures of Don Quixote is completed. The author of the original novel signs himself Cide Hamete Benegeli.

Cervantes tells us plainly that he is not his book's father but its stepfather; the receiver of the story, not the inventor. Throughout the centuries, readers have chosen to disbelieve him. Cervantes composing his book in prison rings truer to us than Cervantes finding a manuscript written by Cide Hamete Benegeli. And yet both statements are fiction and both are true. Cervantes's world (like ours today) is one in which made-up roles are played and masks are worn.

In Cervantes's time, two-thirds of Spain's population, the Muslims and the Jews, had been banished from the peninsula, and only those who converted, or pretended to convert, were allowed to remain under the guise of New Christians. They were known as Moriscos (converted Muslims) and Marranos or Conversos (converted Jews). Religious freedom, which had been guaranteed by the Catholic crown in the capitulation treaties after the taking of Granada in 1492, was rescinded seven years later. Between 1605 (when the first part of *Don Quixote* was published) and 1615 (when the second appeared), the Spanish crown took the decision to expel these New Christians as well, arguing that the conversions were deceitful and spurious. In such a world, appearances take precedence over substance, and perception over fact.

Since prejudice must avoid complexity, the multiplicity of the Arab-speaking people—Arabs of Al-Andalus, Tunisia, Algeria, Morocco, Turkey, the various lands of the Middle East—was reduced to the term "Moors." The Moors, whether long or recently exiled, whether holding on to their beliefs or converted to the faith of Christ, are deemed the enemy, the definition of what a Spanish "Old Christian" is not. Why then would a Spanish writer acknowledge another as the author of his work—and not just any other, but a representative of the people who were banished from his land, people of what was now "the other coast," savages who, in the popular imagination, took their revenge on Christendom by looting and plundering their cities and assaulting the Spanish ships, as those Algerian pirates who held him prisoner for five long years had done?

Such uncertainties are constant in the world of Cide Hamete. His fiction assumes the inconsistency of memory: the famous place in La Mancha whose name will deliberately not be remembered; the uncertain attribution of the characters' surnames (is the old gentleman Alonso

Quixada or Quesada or Quixana? Is Sancho called Panza or Zancas?); the subversion of the conventions of fiction by having Don Quixote and Sancho read about themselves in a Barcelona printing house, thus usurping the identity of the flesh-and-blood reader. Truncated by Cervantes in the midst of an adventure after only eight chapters, interrupted by interpolated stories, essays, and poems, returned to the starting point of the knight's home and set again on the road, the rectilinear narration demanded by an Aristotelian text becomes, according to Cide Hamete himself, a "disheveled, twisted and frayed thread." Reality is faithfully rendered as a succession of approximations and fragments, a chronicle that alternately assumes and disavows the worldview of a madman (Don Quixote) or of someone whom society perceives as mad (Alonso Quijano). It is therefore fitting, even necessary, that the author who presents this reality to us should also be fragmentary and approximate. To describe what is indescribable, the author of *Don Quixote* chooses as his self-portrait the banished one, he who, because he is an outsider, can best perceive that which lies within the society that excludes him. *Don Quixote* is, among many other things, a play of many pairs of shadows: Alonso Quijano and Don Quixote, Don Quixote and Sancho, Aldonsa Lorenzo and Dulcinea, Sancho and Alonso Quijano. To these, Borges added the *Uber-double,* the one who absorbs and opposes them all: Pierre Menard, twentieth-century author of *Don Quixote.*

It is easy to forget that the novel by Cide Hamete that we read is supposed to be a translation; that is to say, a literary work found worthy of being rendered in a language other than the one in which it has been conceived, thereby increasing its readership and augmenting its prestige. In fifteenth- and sixteenth-century Spain, the fact that a book had been translated lent it intellectual cachet. It acknowledged *Don Quixote* as a work of merit, both a mockery and an exaltation of the medieval laws of chivalry that urged its heroes to act justly, no matter what the consequence. And yet, if acting justly in the world can achieve little more than establishing an ideal against the seemingly foregone conclusion of an unjust reality, then writing about such justice becomes itself an act of courage, an attempt to correct God's world through the imagination of good in action.

The laws of chivalry are not themselves the laws of Don Quixote's ethics; chivalry is the form those ethics acquire when performed in the world. However, in Don Quixote's universe, acting according to one's own ethics is not sufficient to play God. Our ethical acts do not have ethical consequences unless they accomplish that which only God can fathom but that we, his instruments, cannot see. A voluntary act of justice does not necessarily lead to justice being done: this is God's domain alone. Here we are in the realm of Qur'anic rather than Christian tradition: the Qur'an says, "Let him that will, take the right path to his Lord. Yet you cannot will, except by the will of God." Don Quixote may be willed by God to believe in justice, but the promise does not extend to the consequences of Don Quixote's actions. Just as Job is allowed endurance to hold the mirror of suffering up to God, Don Quixote holds up to God the mirror of God's own justice.

But is this still true? Our generation wants the writer to be a hero, a star. We want Cervantes to play his role as renegade, as the son of possibly forced converts, as a Stockholm-syndrome captive who learned in the prisons of Algiers to love his Moorish captors and through them the expelled culture of Al-Andalus. We want to see in the alleged authorship of Cide Hamete Benegeli a gesture of restoration or retribution, and in the occasional homages to Arabic culture an act of defiance or of unwillingness to forget. The slurs against the Moors in the book we want to read as realistic features of his characters, like the racist voices in *Heart of Darkness* or the anti-Semitic ones in *The Merchant of Venice*. We want Cervantes to prove to us that in the midst of prejudice, of tyrannical ambition and exclusionary politics, an artist will find ways to voice a protest, to keep the humanitarian banner flying for us readers. We want the author to clear our conscience, we want Cide Hamete to redeem us.

Unfortunately, this may be little more than wishful thinking. It may be that Cervantes attributed *Don Quixote* to Cide Hamete simply as a clever literary device, much like a detective writer chooses the least likely character as the guilty party: not because the choice carries symbolic weight but because, dramatically, it is the most effective. It may be that Cervantes's opinions on the Moorish question were as confused and contradictory as any layman's, and since he was not writing a political tract or a historical account, he did not care about the muddiness of his views as long as the story clipped along nicely. It may be that Cervantes had no inkling that in the distant future his readers would want to know what a writer had to say about his society, and not merely the outcome of his fiction. It may be that Cervantes never guessed that what we mean today by truth is not the intimate wisdom of a tale but the presentation of facts in chronological order within a statistical grid supported by documentary evidence. Writers today complain that they are asked to deliver opinions on everything from food to fashion and from ethics to gender politics. In this vein, we ask writers long dead to comment on these things too—Homer on war, Sophocles on women, Shakespeare on the Jews, Voltaire on civic duties—and then assume that they meant their work to instruct us on all these things. We forget that fiction is neither accountancy nor dogma and does not deliver messages or catechisms. On the contrary, it thrives on ambiguity, in opinions raw or half-baked, in suggestions, intuitions, and emotions.

We can try, of course, to have Cide Hamete speak to us now, in the present, and we can question his pages much as in the Middle Ages readers sought answers in the verses of Virgil, casting the *sortes Virgilianae*. We can make a book converse with us, illuminate us, grant us each the vicarious pleasure of foresight and rebellion, and stand up heroically against the darkness of its time—a stance that would probably have astonished poor Cide Hamete.

Genius, as we well know, seldom manifests itself on the side of the angels, and it is only because we associate great art with virtue that we imagine that great artists are themselves good and virtuous. Whoever Cervantes was, and whatever he might have thought about Spain and its politics, ultimately matters little. More important is the fact that for the readers of *Don Quixote* today, the overwhelming presence of Cide Hamete tells us that a rejected culture will not easily be silenced, that absence in history is as solid as presence, and that literature is often wiser than the wisest of its practitioners.

JOB

The question is: What is he waiting for?

He was, the Holy Book tells us, a perfect and upright man, one who feared God, and eschewed evil. He was married and had seven sons, three daughters, seven thousand sheep, three thousand camels, five hundred yoke of oxen, five hundred she-asses, and a very great number of servants: he was the greatest of all the men of the East. Even though the good fellow would not have hurt a fly, he would rise early in the morning and offer burnt

offerings according to the number of members of his household, just in case one of his children had sinned and cursed God in the heart. "Better to be safe than sorry," Job would say. And so the days and the nights went by pleasantly for Job in his contented old age, surrounded by his family and his cattle, from feast to happy feast and from sacrifice to grateful sacrifice.

So much good behavior got on Satan's nerves, mainly because God would keep mentioning "My servant Job" as proof of the devotion of mankind to his Lordship. "Well, of course," Satan would say. "If you give him everything he wants, little wonder he's thankful. A gorgeous home, great food, slick camels, obedient kids, faithful servants . . . With such bounty, anyone can be good. But let's see what happens if you were to deny him these things."

God could not refuse a challenge and neither did he do things halfway. He told Satan to do whatever he wanted as long as he did not touch Job. Next day, the Sabeans descended on Job's land and stole his oxen and she-asses, a fire from heaven fell down to earth and burned up all Job's sheep, the Chaldeans did away with his camels, and a great wind from the wilderness caused the roof to collapse on Job's children while they were eating and drinking wine, killing them. Hearing of all these awful events, Job blessed the name of the Lord, rent his mantle, shaved his head, and fell down on his knees in an attitude of worship, accepting his fate without saying a single word against his Creator.

God felt terribly pleased and bragged to Satan about the exemplary attitude of his Job. "Did you see how well he behaves, even when I strip from him everything he has?

No regrets, no recriminations." "Sure," Satan admitted. "But that's because he doesn't suffer these things in his own flesh. Put forth your hand now, and touch his bone and his flesh, and he will curse you to your face." Convinced of Job's integrity, God allowed Job to be smitten with sore boils from the sole of his foot to his crown. And even then Job did not utter a single complaint, but merely took a piece of broken pottery to scrape his itchy scabs, and sat down among the ashes. Job's wife could not stand it any longer. "Do something, you fool!" she screamed. But Job remained silent.

His friends (because that's what friends are for) tried to convince him that the divine curse that had fallen on him had a logical explanation, that such things did not happen for no reason, and Job had probably not behaved as impeccably as he appeared to have done. But Job insisted: he had always done what was right, and yet, what mere mortal can grasp the motives that guide the hand of the Almighty?

Maimonides, in his *Guide of the Perplexed,* explained that according to the philosophers (by which he meant Aristotle) God does not and cannot know every little thing that takes place in the human realm, and this for several reasons: because the knowledge of particulars is apprehended by the senses (and God, having no body has no bodily senses); because the particulars are infinite in number (and infinity, by definition, cannot be known even by God); and finally because particulars are the fruit of time and, as they change, God's knowledge of them would have to change as well (and God is not subject to change). Aristotle, says Maimonides, instead of imputing injustice or impotence to God, merely imputes to him ignorance. Job's God allows him to suffer because he does not know the details of Job's suffering, and cannot count every offspring or inspect every camel.

Maimonides then sets out his own point of view. God's divine providence applies only to humans. "Uniquely in this species," Maimonides says, "are all the affairs of individuals, and the good and evil that befall them, in accordance with what they deserve." And he adds: "But as for all other animals, and all the more plants and other things, my opinion is that of Aristotle: that everything that befalls them is, in my view, due to pure chance." God cares about Job's sons and allowed them to be punished for God-knows-what reason. The fate of the camels is not his affair.

For many readers, Job is the model of the perfect citizen. When things go well, he is thankful. When they don't, likewise. He seldom complains, never asks for anything, and, above all, he always allows his Lord and Master to do whatever his Lord and Master fancies. For Job, no unions or workers' guilds, no old-age pensioners associations, no concerned citizens groups, no Amnesty International. Has he lost what was his because of venal Chaldean lawyers? Has his house collapsed because the Sabean real estate agents pocketed a good chunk of the construction budget? Has he fallen ill and the hospital told him his insurance does not cover the required treatment? Is he being exploited at work, do his children disappear in the hands the not-so-secret police? Job bends his head and repeats meekly the bromide about a mere mortal being unable to grasp the reasons that guide the Almighty, and refuses to accuse his Lord and Master.

In the biblical fable, Job wins in the end. The theologian Jack Miles suggests that when all is said and done, Job has managed to silence God. God (the God of the book of Job) never speaks again. Recognizing that Job has triumphed over all the deliberate adversities, God silently decides to reward his servant's great devotion and grants Job twice what he had taken from him. That is the happy ending.

But in real life, things are somewhat different. Job continues to suffer without a reward in sight. The question is: How long will Job endure? How many more things will have to be taken from him before he recognizes that these acts of injustice are utterly unacceptable? At what point will he ask, like a Roman lawyer, *Cui bono,* whom does all this benefit? Who has kept his cattle, his land, the fruit of his labors? Who is responsible for the death of his children? When does a man have the obligation to defend himself against the arbitrary decisions of those in power? Of how many more rights will he have to be stripped before Job says, "Enough already"?

Satan's bet is still on.

QUASIMODO

Sometime in the 1930s, a wealthy Argentinian matron was strolling in the park of Palermo, in downtown Buenos Aires, when she suddenly noticed an old beggar woman. A remarkable feature of the park is its rose garden, and the lady delighted in walking there every morning, admiring the colors and the scent of the flowers. The sight of the beggar, with her warty face, yellow teeth, and bulbous nose, offended her. Therefore, in order not to see the ugly features again, she offered the beggar a weekly fee to stay

out of the elegant garden. Proud of her action, the curious philanthropist said in the press that she had done it "in defense of beauty." This should not surprise us: in the late nineteenth century, the so-called "ugly laws" in the United States prohibited individuals with physical deformities from visiting public spaces, and in several cities these laws remained in effect until the 1970s. However enlightened we might think ourselves to be, privately or publicly we deem ugliness a crime.

Ugliness, like beauty in the old tag, is in the eye of the beholder. This variation on *esse est percipi* is no doubt true, but ugliness is also a concept born of our sense of necessary opposites. Aristotle, in the *Metaphysics,* noted that the principal characteristics of beauty are "order, symmetry, and definiteness"; we therefore may adduce that those of ugliness are disorder, asymmetry, and vagueness.

The great paradox of aesthetics is that (perhaps out of a stubborn contrariness) we try to look at what is conventionally labeled beautiful or ugly from a viewpoint that contradicts the earned assumptions: a beautiful face as tediously regular, inexpressive, or trite; an ugly one as interesting, experienced, *jolie laide.* Many cultures uglify beauty and beautify ugliness. Navajo rug weavers and Amish quilters, Islamic calligraphers and Turkish ship-builders all deliberately incorporate imperfections or (as one scholar calls them) "controlled accidents" in their work that show the skill of the artist and also the belief that what is perfect belongs only to the Godhead. Japanese potters embrace the concept of *wabi-sabi,* which, as Crispin Sartwell explains, sees beauty in "the withered, weathered, tarnished, scarred, intimate, coarse, earthy, evanescent, tentative, ephemeral," thereby not only undermining conventional notions of what is pleasing but forcing spectators to alter their traditional perceptions. Socrates' famous ugliness is transformed through dialogue into intellectual beauty that will not decay like the beauty of the body; this conceptual change elicits the question of whether it is fair to judge something or someone by a single, constraining set of parameters only.

If such seemingly simple notions—what is ugly, what is beautiful—vary to such a vast degree, perhaps our entire panoply of judgmental certainties should come into question. Not, of course, in an indiscriminate sweeping-out of all values, but as a more careful consideration of how cultural teachings, private experience, and accepted conventions fashion our eye and our palate. "Ask a toad what is beauty," wrote Voltaire, "and he will answer that it is his female, with two large round eyes sticking out of her head."

Of all the ugly faces that haunt the pages of our books, perhaps the one whose nature is the least definable is that of the Hunchback of Notre-Dame, Victor Hugo's Quasimodo. Faced with the ugliness of his features, his author confesses himself vanquished. "We shall not try to give the reader an idea of that tetrahedral nose, that horseshoe mouth, that little left eye half-hidden behind a reddish, bushy, bristling eyebrow, while the right eye is entirely concealed under an enormous wart; of those teeth in disarray, broken here and there like the embattled parapet of a fortress; of that callous lip upon which one of these teeth encroaches like the tusk of an elephant; of that forked chin; and above all, of the expression spread over the whole, a mixture of malice, amazement, and distress. Let the readers dream of this whole, if they can."

That is what we have done: dreamt him. Not only since Hugo's novel was published in 1831, but even long before then, since our earliest nightmares, when primitive Quasimodos roamed the troglodyte villages frightening the hunters of mammoths. If what the book of Genesis says is true, then Quasimodo was made in the image of a horrible Jehovah, terror of his angels and demons. Today Quasimodo is that other who returns our features in a warped looking glass; the person we try not to be, not to offer as our self to the world. We primp ourselves, we array and adorn and comb ourselves, we put on makeup and disguise ourselves in order not to show any features that others might not like. We know, as Bishop Berkeley explained, that we only exist in the perceiving eye.

Hamlet's question is not Quasimodo's: Quasimodo simply wants to be allowed to be. He wants to have the same rights as others, to enjoy the changing seasons, the company of friends, the contemplation of beauty. He asks not to be made subservient to appearances, to be allowed to be able to act according to his emotions and thoughts, and not as a mirror for the horror of others. He does not want to be the incarnation of alien fears. Like the Daring Young Man on the Flying Trapeze in William Saroyan's story, he might think of writing *An Application for Permission to Live.* He does not.

The contradiction between what lies within and what stands without, between what is visible and what is hidden, is a literary commonplace, and yet we continue to be deceived by it when we encounter this contradiction in real life. The mellowness of the eyes that are revealed to belong to Klaus Barbie, the stern frown and mean lips in the portraits of Mother Teresa, the ridiculous mustache and the idiotic look of both Hitler and Charlie Chaplin teach us very little. We continue to believe that a face like Quasimodo's can harbor nothing good.

And yet, as far as he himself is concerned, Quasimodo is the opposite of his physical appearance. Like the lovely flowers he shows to Esmeralda in the earthen pot (which in his grotesque metaphorical mind are an image of himself) so that she may compare them to the wilted flowers in the cut-crystal vase (image of his rival, Captain Phoebus), Quasimodo knows that his beauty is internal and that no one makes the effort to see it. He can be loving, generous, brave, he can show himself grateful (even, at least in the beginning, towards the fanatical Archdeacon Frollo) or in love (increasingly so, towards Esmeralda). None of these things matter. He is monstrously ugly, and that defines him, the way colossal beauty defines the building that lends its name to the novel. This is a dangerous notion, this hint of a hidden truth. If underneath the hump, the crooked teeth, the twisted eyes Quasimodo is an excellent fellow, then what lies beneath the exquisitely carved stones and the stained-glass windows of Notre Dame?

Twenty-five years after the publication of the novel, Hugo asked the same question in *Les contemplations:*

> A word can burst from the hideous hole;
> Don't ask which. If the pit be the mouth,
> Dear God, what then is the voice?

CASAUBON

Mr. Casaubon is a bookworm, a prisoner in his ivory tower, a literary gentleman of no particular spark, a reader for whom the real world does not exist except as an intrusion in his study. He is (according to Mrs. Cadwallader) "a great bladder for dried peas to rattle in," a pedant who delivers himself with finicky precision "as if he had been called upon to make a public statement." No one would say that he is handsome. Dorothea Brooke's friends call him a mummy, point out with disgust the two white

moles with hairs growing out of them that adorn his face, and compare his sallow complexion to that of a *cochon de lait.* He is the incarnation of every cliché society hurls at the intellectual: reclusive, misanthropic, the contrary of sexy. From the humanists' Book Fool in the fifteenth century to Superman's alter ego (Clark Kent) and Roald Dahl's Matilda in our time, the timid scholar, the librarian, or simply the reader has been depicted as a bumbling, glasses-wearing nerd, someone to be mocked in the public eye. When Jo, in *Little Women,* delivers her freshly written stories to the magazine she hopes will publish them, she does it furtively: she is afraid of being mocked for her efforts, and even when she confides in her friend Laurie, she swears him to secrecy. The Egyptian philosopher Hypatia (both in real life and in Charles Kingsley's novel of that name) is murdered by an intolerant mob. Julien Sorel, at the beginning of *Le Rouge et le noir,* is beaten by his father for reading a book. Jo and Hypatia and Julien and Mr. Casaubon all know that the big bustling world has no respect for the intellectual act.

The young Doctor Lydgate, for instance, is praxis to the Reverend Edward Casaubon's derided logos. Lydgate possesses "a voice habitually deep and sonorous, yet capable of becoming very low and gentle at the right moment." He does not profess bravery but acknowledges "a good deal of pleasure" in fighting. He is not only a man of action: when he stops doing whatever he is doing, he is apt to pick up a book, Samuel Johnson's *Rasselas* or *Gulliver's Travels,* for example, but a dictionary will do, or the Bible, as long as it has the Apocrypha in it. Something he must read when he is not riding or running and hunting or listening to the talk of other men. It is said of him that he can do anything he likes, but that he certainly has not yet liked to do anything remarkable. He is a vigorous animal with a ready understanding, but no spark has kindled in him a true intellectual passion; knowledge seems to him a very superficial affair, easily mastered. Unlike Lydgate, the Reverend Casaubon knows that the essence of intellectual pursuits lies in their difficulty.

Before Dorothea Brooke meets Casaubon for the first time, she feels towards the unknown scholar "some venerating expectation." Casaubon is noted as "a man of profound learning, understood for many years to be engaged on a great work concerning religious history; also as a man of wealth enough to give lustre to his piety, and having views of his own which were to be more clearly ascertained on the publication of his book." His very name (echoing that of the great sixteenth-century scholar Isaac Casaubon) carries an impressiveness hard to measure without a precise chronology of scholarship. After meeting him, Dorothea feels that he is the most interesting man she has ever seen. Desdemona thought the same of the Moor who wooed her with fantastic tales of adventure.

Edward Casaubon is a man entirely devoted to this great work. His ambitious *Key to All Mythologies* (his never-to-be-completed magnum opus) antecedes James Frazier's *The Golden Bough* by six decades and Joseph Campbell's *The Hero with a Thousand Faces* by more than a century. Had it been finished, it would probably have placed Casaubon among the greatest scholars of all time. As a clergyman, Casaubon sees Christian revelation mirrored in every civilization from the beginning of our histories, but distorted in imperfect mirrors that still reflect certain essential and universal truths. Casaubon is a poststructuralist. George Eliot, devotee of German pragmatism, appears skeptical of the intellectual capacities of her character and describes Mr. Casaubon's theory of the elements as something "not likely to bruise itself unawares against discoveries: it floated among flexible conjectures." And adds: "It was as free from interruption as a plan for threading the stars together." George Eliot derides constellations.

The Reverend Casaubon wishes to find a soulmate who will also be a helpmate in the great project to which he has devoted his life, someone on a quest for a transcendent truth. Casaubon has been accused of merely wanting a slave, a mindless drudge to tidy up after him, but that is not at all the case. In what Borges considered one of the best detective novels ever written, Eden Philpotts's *The Red Redmaynes*, the protagonist's thoughts on the ideal mate are given in the following terms: "Mark Brendon was old-fashioned and the women born of the war attracted him not at all. He recognized their fine qualities and often their distinction of mind; yet his ideal struck backward to another and earlier type—the type of his own mother who, as a widow, had kept house for him until her death. She was his feminine ideal—restful, sympathetic, trustworthy—one who always made his interests hers, one who concentrated upon his life rather than her own and found in his progress and triumphs the core of her own existence." Casaubon does want Dorothea to make his interests hers, but only if she can work with him, side by side, not as a servant but as an intelligent assistant. Casaubon wants Dorothea to concentrate upon her own life, even if he has definite ideas about the direction in which her life should most properly evolve.

Why does Dorothea marry Edward Casaubon? Because she believes him to be a man who can understand the higher inward life and with whom there could be some spiritual communion, someone who could illuminate principles with the widest knowledge, a man whose learning almost amounts to a proof of whatever he believed. So when her uncle lets her know of the Reverend's intentions, she accepts gladly. "It would be a great honour to any one to be his companion."

But would it necessarily be a great honor for anyone to be Dorothea's companion? Sure, she enjoys partaking of intellectual discussions and learning about history and art, but only up to a certain point: that point reached, she becomes bored. In moments of distress, Dorothea finds that books are of no use, even thinking is of no use. Alas for the much-desired marriage of true minds! In the often quoted final paragraph of the novel, Dorothea is described as one of "the number who lived faithfully a hidden life, and rest in unvisited tombs." Admirable, no doubt. And yet, what kind of devotion would be required to relinquish a scholarly, artistic, or intellectual pursuit for such a mild, easily bored person? When Casaubon, halfway through the novel, on the day before his fatal heart attack, asks Dorothea to promise him she will comply with his (unspecified) wishes after his death, she feels unable to do so, because, as she believes, there is a deep difference between the devotion to the living and the indefinite promise of devotion to the dead. If she consented, she feels, it would be as if she were saying "Yes" to her own doom. "No!" she decides. "If you die, I will put no finger to your work." So much for her earlier desire to provide intellectual companionship. Obviously, she has the right to discover that this is not the best life for her, but what about her promises?

During their honeymoon in Rome, Dorothea learns that Casaubon does not wish to take advantage of her offer to help him in his research at the Vatican archives. But Dorothea believes her husband's true intentions to be other. "Surely I am in a strangely selfish weak state of mind," she says to herself. "How can I have a husband who is so much above me without knowing that he needs me less than I need him?" But that is the whole point. W. H. Auden put it this way: "If equal affections cannot be / Let the more loving one be me." This is Casaubon, and he would have been horrified to discover how little his wife understood it. Whatever the author's own opinions might be, we quickly notice that Casaubon is lovingly protective (perhaps overly so) towards Dorothea. Dorothea, however, feels that she's living a "nightmare of a life in which every energy was arrested by dread." But what does Casaubon feel? According to Eliot, "Poor Mr Casaubon was distrustful of everyone's feelings towards him, especially as a husband. To let any one suppose that he was jealous would be to admit their (suspected) view of his disadvantages: to let them know that he did not find marriage particularly blissful would imply his conversion to their (probably) earlier disapproval." It would be as bad, she says, as letting his fellow scholars know how backward he was in organizing his *Key to All Mythologies.* Mr. Ramsay in *To the Lighthouse* believes that the progress of human thought can be followed in alphabetical order, each successive concept represented by a letter, and has diligently thought his way through from A to Q; he will not, however, reach R. Flaubert's two buffoons Bouvard and Pécuchet will never come to the end of their universal encyclopedia. Likewise, Mr. Casaubon will not complete his colossal *Key.* These intellectual Babels are, in their very essence, unaccomplishable tasks. Kafka wrote: "If it had been possible to build the Tower of Babel without ascending it, the work would have been permitted."

However, in spite of dreading all these projects that might, because impossible, become tiresome instead of helpful, Dorothea is grateful for small mercies, such as Mr. Casaubon's offering to teach her languages. But it is not out of devotion to her future husband that she wishes to know Latin and Greek. Those "provinces of masculine knowledge," as she calls them, seem to her a standing ground from which all truth could be seen more truly. This is the fixed point that Saint Teresa of Avila (with whom Eliot compares her) sought in her road towards perfection. In this sense, Saint Teresa was closer in her sense of spiritual duty to the Reverend Casaubon than to Dorothea. Because, unlike Saint Teresa, Dorothea is constantly doubting her own conclusions and lamenting her own ignorance. "How could she be confident that one-roomed cottages were not for the glory of God," Eliot writes, "when men who knew the classics appeared to conciliate indifference to the cottages with zeal for the glory?" Casaubon's goal is the pursuit of knowledge in itself, the achievement of which, in its fullest measure, lies always beyond the horizon. Had she persevered in her own quest for knowledge, realizing as he does that the enterprise is essentially inexhaustible and yet still worth pursuing, Dorothea might have had the shadow of an answer.

SATAN

Whether what we call consciousness was born of what we call imagination, or whether it was the other way round, at the very beginning of the human age we began telling stories to attempt to explain our existence, and we dreamt up a divine being, a magic word, a dragon, a tortoise, a collision of matter and antimatter to be our "Once upon a time." Pascal accused Descartes of requiring a "little shove" kindly provided by a primordial

Creator, who then is no longer needed; after that, stories can unfold on their own.

The scandal effected by Judaism in reducing the many ancient gods to a single omnipresent and omniscient divinity must have felt too lopsided for a humanity accustomed to a Pythagorean binary universe. Everything we conceive has an underbelly, and soon a second character was brought onto the scriptural stage. He too was omniscient and omnipresent, even if ultimately subject to the divine will, and yet sufficiently crafty to tempt even the Almighty, as in the cautionary tales of Job and of God's Son in the desert. He was darkness to God's light, a destructive force opposed to his creative energy, an alternative truth to the Truth. He was given many names, among them Satan, Lucifer, Mephistopheles, Beelzebub, Mastema (in early rabbinical texts), Iblis (in the Qur'an), or simply the Devil (from the Greek *diabolos,* meaning "slanderer"). In the book of Jubilees (which is part of the Apocrypha) it is told that when Jehovah decided to expel the rebel angels after the Flood and release humankind from temptation, Satan persuaded God to agree to allow him to retain 10 percent of the punished flock in order to continue to test, as if they were lab rats, the faith of humans. Because of Satan's ability to deceive, Jesus called him "the Father of Lies" (which is also the definition of a novelist).

Not content with this absolute division between the Supreme Good and the Supreme Bad, the Sufi poet Al-Ghazali imagined an alibi for Satan and wrote that when the angels, at the bidding of God, prostrated themselves in front of the newly created Adam, only Satan refused, saying that God's bid was a test, because "Heaven forbid that anyone worship anyone except the One Almighty." Al-Ghazali does not say how God rewarded his faithful servant. Four centuries after Al-Ghazali, the Egyptian scholar Shihab al-Din al-Nuwayri reported that after the creation of Adam, Satan said to the other angels, "If the Lord prefers this creature to me, then I will rebel against Him. And if He prefers me to it, then I will destroy it." Because, Satan explained, "I am better than it: He created me of fire, but it out of clay."

In other religions, Satan continues to be the unrelenting enemy of humankind. In *The City of God,* Augustine saw him as deliberately setting a bad example, and argued that when "man lives according to man, not according to God, he is like the devil [Satan]." A century earlier, the Gnostic philosopher Apelles said that the Evil One was a demiurge who had inspired the Old Testament prophets. Dante wisely placed Satan in the center of the earth, where this most beautiful of angels fell after his rebellion, transformed into an ugly three-faced monster and causing the lands of the Southern Hemisphere to retreat in horror, leaving in their place an aquatic world *senza gente,* "without people." Martin Luther (like Saint Anthony before him) saw Satan as a bully and a nuisance, and threw an inkwell at him, causing a stain on the wall of the study in Wartburg Castle that could still be seen up to a century ago. Milton imagined Satan as a sort of Möbius strip ("Which way I fly is hell; myself am hell"). Goethe, with a pinch of compassion, suggested that Satan tempts humans because he is miserable and "solamen miseris socios habuisse doloris" (misery seeks companions.) Late Qur'anic exegetes noted that Satan, when he tempted

Eve, took on not the form of a serpent but of a beautiful camel with "a multi-coloured tail, red, yellow, green, white, black, a mane of pearl, hair of topaz, eyes like the planets Venus and Jupiter, and an aroma like musk blended with ambergris."

No doubt Satan (or his image) is still among us. Up to this day, in Austria, Bavaria, Croatia, the Czech Republic, Hungary, Slovakia, Slovenia, and parts of northern Italy, Satan (known in these region as the Krampus) accompanies Father Christmas on his rounds, looking to shove naughty children into a sack and thrash them with bundles of birch. The Krampus-Satan is an ugly horned creature that predates Christianity, carrying chains to show that now he is bound to the will of the church. On other occasions, Satan has taken on the appearance of a poodle, a viper, a dragon, or even a gentleman.

Dante (again) argued that everything in the universe is the fruit of God's love, including sin. Following this idea, Satan can be seen as the perverter or diverter of the divine projection, causing humans to love in excess (lust or avarice) or not enough (envy, sloth, and anger), or to direct their love towards inappropriate objects (covetousness and pride).

Saint Bonaventure wrote that our bewilderment when confronted with inexplicable suffering merely shows our lack of faith in the perfect justice of God, and stems from our not being aware of the whole story (as when we judge Lord Jim a coward or Romeo a mere flirt after reading only the first pages of their adventures). We resort to Satan to try to understand the infamous events that plague us daily, now and always. Satan (we say) whispers horrible things in our ears and inspires our worst deeds. It is Satan (we insist) who is responsible for disease, war, famine; for the rise to power of Caligula, Goebbels, Videla; for torture, murder, and the abuse of children. Satan is the hazy excuse for our nightmarish actions and bloodthirsty dreams. Unfortunately, the argument for his responsibility is ultimately unconvincing.

If the work of Satan can be seen as the dark side of the labors of God, the all-pervading misery of the world might be understood as a certain dearth of divine energy, as the inconceivable exhaustion of the Almighty, fed up with his imperfect creations. The Hasidim tell the following story. In an obscure village in central Poland, there was a small synagogue. One night, when making his rounds, the rabbi entered and saw God sitting in a dark corner. The rabbi fell upon his face and cried out, "Lord God, what are you doing here?" God answered him neither in thunder nor out of a whirlwind, but with a small voice: "I am tired, Rabbi, I am tired unto death."

THE HiPPOGRiFF

Among the many kings, queens, noblemen and ladies, pirates, servants, magicians, allegorical incarnations, and mythological beasts that populate the forty-six cantos of Ariosto's *Orlando Furioso,* one in particular crosses magnificently unscathed the entire poem. He appears for the first time, unnamed and in full flight, in the second canto, described simply as "a horse with wings," mounted by the (also then unnamed) magician Atlante; he disappears in one of the last cantos of the poem now glorified by his

own and his rider's actions, freed by the knight Astolfo,
following the orders of no less an authority than Saint
John the Evangelist. In his exalted career, the hippogriff
accomplishes many illustrious deeds and undertakes many
a dangerous journey across the earth, as well as to the
moon. In the end who cannot but feel that his freedom
is much deserved? We cheer him on.

We think we know what a hippogriff looks like.
Ariosto, to prevent any dismissive notion of the noble
creature as fiction, tells us straightforwardly, in the fourth
canto:

> His steed was not a fiction, but instead
> The offspring of a griffin and a mare.
> Its plumage, forefeet, muzzle, wings, and head
> Like those of its paternal parent were.
> The rest was from its dam inherited.
> It's called a hippogriff. Such beasts, though rare,
> In the Rhiphaean mountains, far beyond
> The icy waters of the north, are found.

The "though rare" is important, implying that beasts
such as these are seldom seen by human eyes. But seldom
is not never. Virgil had already announced, in one of his
eclogues, that griffins would mate with mares, an unlikely
event since, ancient commentators noted, griffins and
horses are mortal enemies. Virgil mentions the mating to
imply that such a time will never come, but these rhetorical devices have a way of proving us wrong. Pairing
griffins with horses, even in poetry, lends the imaginary
beast the factual reality of a domestic animal.

Ariosto saw these things. He realized that even if such

splendid occurrences could not be frequent, even one such offspring would suffice for the inner truth of his story. "No magic creature, like the rest," he writes, dismissing other magical inventions, "But real and true, a prodigy of Nature." How can we doubt so vehement a testimony?

The hippogriff is both singular and universal. In spite of his rarity, he belongs to the bestiary of permissible creatures. So strong is his imaginary verisimilitude that far from being unique, like the phoenix (of which only one can exist in the world at a time), he has become a frequent creature in the imagination, and after his flight into freedom at the end of Ariosto's poem, he has found new settings for new adventures. Since a horse that is dragonish rather than merely winged seems better suited to fight a common sea monster, the hippogriff replaced his cousin, the simple Pegasus, in depictions of Perseus and Andromeda, who in turn became Ariosto's Ruggiero and Angelica, as in the painting by Ingres. Because a runaway horse is not wonderful enough for the magical realm of Calderón's *Life Is a Dream,* the first lines of the play address not a mere nag but a "violent hippogriff who runs as fast as the wind," and who has thrown Princess Rosaura off her saddle and into the world of dreams. Since the hippogriff has acquired an aristocratic prestige, being far less common than a zombie or a werewolf, over the past century fantasy writers have introduced this endangered species into their realms, from E. R. Eddison in *The Worm Ouroboros,* to J. K. Rowling in her *Harry Potter* saga.

But there is something else.

René Magritte, commenting on his painting *The*

Elective Affinities, notes that though we know that birds normally occupy a birdcage, the image becomes more interesting if instead of a bird we see a fish or a shoe behind those bars. "But though these images are very strange," Magritte goes on to say, "they are unhappily accidental, arbitrary. However, it is possible to obtain a new image which will stand up to examination because it has something final, something just right about it. And this is the image of an egg in a cage." Something *juste,* says Magritte; that is the quality of Ariosto's hippogriff.

The vast narrative jumble that is the *Orlando Furioso,* with its battles and friendships and feuds and passionate undertakings, is, above all, juste. Everything in this hallucinatory story, more populous than almost any other epic narrative (including *The Lord of the Rings*) and certainly one of the most entertaining, strikes, in the discriminating mind, a consistently right note. At every step, Ariosto could have chosen a different turn, another twist, allowed a scene to prolong itself or to be cut short. It is not psychological or historical or even narrative coherence that holds the story together, far less any classical notions of place and time. The rhyming fragments that make up the forty-six long cantos of the poem, driving the reader from hilltops to vales, from castles to seas, from the earth to the moon and back, never seem "unhappily accidental, arbitrary." A wild poetic logic governs the adventures, a logic faithfully suited to the mad fury of its hero. Emblematic of this is the hippogriff, an impossibility born of an impossibility, as reasonable as a dream within a dream.

CAPTAIN NEMO

Nemo. Nadie. Niemand. Nessuno. The identity that denies itself begins, in the West, almost universally with the letter *N.* Johann Gottlieb Fichte imagined a philosophical distinction between Someone, *aliquis* in Latin, defined as an I that is present, and Nobody, *nemo,* a non-I, a lack of existence incarnate, a sort of black hole of one's being. Odysseus chose this latter identity and told the thick-headed Cyclops that his name was Nobody: the nominal absence was his salvation. Nemo is also the name

Jules Verne gave to his famous seafaring rebel, precursor of the Greenpeace warriors, anarchist terrorist avant la lettre.

But who is Captain Nemo?

Confident, with deep black eyes that can scan at one glance a quarter of the horizon, cold, pale, energetic, courageous, proud, aged somewhere between thirty-five and fifty, tall, with an ample forehead, a straight nose, clearly shaped lips, magnificent teeth, long and delicate hands proper for a noble and impassioned soul: this is how Captain Nemo presents himself to the aghast Professor Aronnax in the bowels of the *Nautilus* submarine. Pierre-Jules Hetzel, publisher of *Twenty Thousand Leagues Under the Sea* and all the other great Jules Verne novels, recognized in Nemo a portrait of his creator and instructed the illustrator, Edouard Riou, to use Verne as a model for the book's hero.

Nemo is a fighter, a nonconformist, an idealist, in the sense that the nineteenth century gave this last word, nowadays so demeaned. Nemo is also a reader. After a curious meal in which the several dishes served are proven to be strange marine delicacies cleverly disguised, Nemo invites his captive guest to visit his underwater residence. The first room into which Nemo leads him is the library. "Tall, black-rosewood bookcases, inlaid with copperwork, held on their wide shelves a large number of uniformly bound books. These furnishings followed the contours of the room, their lower parts leading to huge couches upholstered in maroon leather and curved for maximum comfort. Light, movable reading-stands, which could be pushed away or pulled near as desired, allowed books to be positioned on them for easy study. In the center stood a huge table covered with pamphlets, among which some newspapers, long out of date, were visible. Electric light flooded this harmonious whole, falling from four frosted half globes set in the scrollwork of the ceiling." Professor Aronnax expresses his admiration of this library that has accompanied its reader down into the farthest depths of the ocean; a collection, the professor says, "that would do credit to more than one continental palace." But Captain Nemo will not admit that his library has anything out-landish about it. "Where could one find greater silence or solitude, professor?" he asks his guest. For Nemo (as for us) silence and solitude are two essential attributes of an authentic library, whose ideal reader, divided into an in-finity of characters made up of words, is always Nobody.

The library of Captain Nemo contains some twelve thousand books of science, ethics, and fiction, written in many languages. Three characteristics define it. In the first place, there are no books of political economy, since no theory in this field satisfies its demanding reader. In the second, the order of Nemo's books seems arbitrary, min-gling subjects and languages without any apparent logic, as if the Captain liked to read whatever chance put in front of him. In the third, there are no new books on these submarine shelves.

These twelve thousand books, the Captain explains, are his "sole remaining ties with dry land. But I was done with the shore the day my *Nautilus* submerged for the first time under the waters. That day I purchased my last volumes, my last pamphlets, my last newspapers, and ever since I've chosen to believe that humanity no longer thinks or writes. In any event, professor, these books are at your disposal, and you may use them freely." Recognizing on one of the shelves Joseph Bertrand's *Founders of Astronomy,* published in 1865, Professor Aronnax realizes that Captain Nemo's underwater life must have begun barely three years earlier. We are in 1868, two years before the date on which Verne's novel appeared.

If every library is autobiographical, then Captain Nemo's reveals something of the hidden identity of its reader. The surface world, the world of chaotic human society, appalls the Captain. He prefers the seclusion of his *Nautilus.* He believes in the spirit of invention, in the ethical imagination, in the endless curiosity of the human being. He loathes its excesses, its taste for tyranny, its bloodthirsty greed. He cares, above all, for freedom, but not any freedom. It would not be surprising to find among the books of the *Nautilus* library Pierre-Joseph Proudhon's *Solution to the Social Problem,* a volume Verne knew well. "It is not Freedom subjected to Order, as in the case of the constitutional monarchy; nor is it Freedom representing Order," Proudhon wrote in an allegorical vein. "It is reciprocal Freedom, not limited Freedom. Freedom is not the daughter but the mother of Order." This life-giving freedom, Proudhon called "Positive Anarchy." That is Nemo's belief as well, except that he does not content himself with Proudhon's idealistic proposal. Nemo is, one could argue, the precursor of those violent nineteenth-century anarchists—Ravachol, Auguste Vaillant, Émil Henry, Santo Caserio—whose system of belief was translated into bombs and assassinations. Obviously, the deliberate shipwrecks caused by the *Nautilus* are another version of such terrorist acts.

Captain Nemo's violence in the second part of the novel frightened Hetzel. Answering the publisher's objections, Verne explained that according to the rules of fiction, things could not have taken place otherwise. The taciturn bibliophile who shows Professor Aronnax "the loveliest productions of the human spirit" becomes in the necessary moment of action not a teacher of humankind but "its sombre executioner." Books have served Nemo as guides towards knowledge and as a sampler of humankind's shared experience, but (as readers know) a book, or even an entire library, can only illuminate the path a reader has chosen; it cannot direct that reader towards an obligatory goal, or even impose a certain direction. Years later, Verne would tell the story of the end of his hero in *The Mysterious Island,* in which the disillusioned anarchist accepts his defeat. "Loneliness, isolation: these are sad things, beyond the reach of human strength," says Nemo in his agony. "I die of having thought it possible to live alone!"

Verne's grandson Jean-Jules Verne explained that his grandfather wanted to write about the struggle of the Polish people against the Russian Empire but that, perhaps because of the French government's censorship, he never did. Instead he wrote *Twenty Thousand Leagues Under the Sea.* Captain Nemo is a universal, not a specific revolutionary. He will be known "as a great criminal," he explains with a haughty smile. "Yes, a rebel, perhaps an outlaw against humanity!" But to Professor Aronnax he says, "I'm the law, I'm the tribunal!" And pointing to the vessel he intends to attack, he adds, "I'm the oppressed, and there are my oppressors! Thanks to them, I've witnessed the destruction of everything I loved, cherished, and venerated—homeland, wife, children, father, and mother! There lies everything I hate!"

After the terrible scene of destruction that follows, Professor Aronnax tries to fall asleep and cannot. In his imagination, he sees the story from the beginning, as if he were leafing through a book he has already read. As Aronnax recalls the recent past days, Captain Nemo ceases to be his equal and is transformed into "a creature of the deep waters, a spirit of the seas." Before our readers' eyes, Professor Aronnax, a character in Verne's novel, becomes the reader of his own adventures. Now Nemo is no longer a man like Aronnax himself but something vaster, less comprehensible, more terrifying, not restricted to Verne's imagination but belonging to the universal library. At this magical point, protagonist and author, author and reader, reader and protagonist blend into a single being, both inside and outside the book, suspended in the time of the telling and our own time, when we read him today.

FRANKENSTEIN'S MONSTER

Pythagorean tradition decreed that every creature has or will have, now or in the future, something of another. "Every man is not only himself," wrote Sir Thomas Browne, "there hath been many Diogenes and as many Timons, though but few of that name: men are liv'd over again, the world is now as it was in Ages past; there was none then, but there hath been some one since that parallels him, and is, as it were, his revived self."

No one better embodies this ancient notion than the

creature born (if the verb is permissible) "one sad November night" towards the end of the eighteenth century,
in the German town of Ingolstadt. He has no name. He
comes into the world already an adult, made up of a
variety of human members and organs, chosen because
of their athletic proportions and their classical beauty, in
the dissecting theater of the university and also in the
basements of the morgue. The result, as his creator himself confesses, is not what he hoped for: the ensemble of
human bits, once brought to life, does not retain the
perfection of each of its parts. "His yellow skin scarcely
covered the work of muscles and arteries beneath; his hair
was of a lustrous black, and flowing; his teeth of a pearly
whiteness; but these luxuriances only formed a more horrid contrast with his watery eyes, that seemed almost of
the same colour as the dun-white sockets in which they
were set, his shrivelled complexion and straight black lips."

Dr. Frankenstein's wish is to create life without the
participation of a woman. Creation from male seed alone
is the alchemist's purpose, the patriarchal dream, the mad
scientist's goal. From the Jewish golems to the animated
sculptures of fable and science—Eve made out of Adam's
rib, Pygmalion's ivory woman, Gepetto's wooden Pinocchio, the eighteenth- and early-nineteenth-century auto-
mata that so enchanted Mary Shelley and her circle—men
have imagined themselves capable of creating life without
female assistance: that is to say, by depriving women of
their exclusive power to conceive. No women take part in
Dr. Frankenstein's creation of the Monster: it is an affair
conducted solely by a male. For the medieval theologians,
the attempt at conception without male-female coupling

was a terrible sin. According to the sixteenth-century Spanish scholar Rabbi Moses Cordovero, "The union and coupling of man and woman is a sign of coupling from on high," and any diversion from this consecrated method is a denial of the will of God. In attempting to create life from dead body parts, Dr. Frankenstein is sinning against God's omnipotence.

There is, however, another side to the myth: the plight of the Monster itself. Like Adam the sufferer, he is a piece of living clay that never asked to be brought into this world. At its rawest, most primordial, the creature is a Golem, a wooden doll granted life; at its most exalted it is Hamlet praising himself as a wondrous piece of work, Segismundo wondering whether he is not merely a shape in a dream. This agony, this ecstasy are both revealed in the Monster's awful face, which we know from the films, a face that, like that of Garbo, is one of the indisputable icons of our time. Garbo's face, with its disturbing classic features, is that of Dante's Beatrice, the "radiant visage that receives our soulful longings," the reflection of that part of ourselves which Westerners associate with spiritual beauty and transcendental wisdom. ("Think of nothing," the director Rouben Mamoulian is said to have instructed Garbo when she asked him how to play the unforgettable final shot of *Queen Christina*. That vacuum was made for us, the audience, an empty space in which to lose ourselves.) The Monster's face is its counterpart, its shadow, the face of our subhuman self, bearing the features we fear will one day emerge from a distracted mirror—the face in Dorian Gray's picture, the face of the wicked Mr. Hyde. If Garbo's face is divinely empty, the Monster's face is demonically full, bursting at its visible seams with that which we wish to conceal. It is not "evil" (just as Garbo's is not "good") but execrable (as Garbo's is immaculate). Thanks to the inventive hand of the makeup artist Jack Pierce, it is more than that of any other humanoid monster. It is a face dreamed up by someone who knows what a face should be but cannot quite manage to contain it, a mistaken face, a face so big that it grips us with the fear that if we were to come close to it (in Chesterton's words) "the face would be too big to be possible." It is a perfect failure of a face, an anonymous mock-version of the biblical face made in God's own image. When Boris Karloff assumed the Monster's face, his name in the credits was replaced by a question mark.

The Monster created by Dr. Victor Frankenstein is (no one denies this, not even his own father) of an unbearable ugliness. Seeing him fills one with fear, and confronted with the fear he provokes, the Monster attacks or defends himself. He can live among humans only on condition of not being seen, a state of being which (as Bishop Berkeley explained) denies itself and becomes one of inexistence. The Monster can learn how humans live because the old hermit who receives him in his house is blind; he can study world history through Volney's *Ruins of Empire* because the young Swiss man who reads the pompous text aloud does not know that the Monster is hidden outside the window. When he is discovered, he is pursued like a marked prey, and no one asks whether he is innocent or culpable. The Monster is the model victim: guiltless and maligned, he is goaded into committing acts of violence. Like any victim, he wants to know why he is hated. He is not himself responsible for his presence in the world, as one of the epigraphs of the novel, taken from Milton's *Paradise Lost,* makes clear: "Did I request thee, Maker, from my clay to mould me man? Did I solicit thee from darkness to promote me?" The fruit of an ambitious madman or of a careless inventor, the Monster shares his hard fate with Adam; that is to say, with all of us. And yet, in spite of his suffering, he does not want to die. "Life," he says to his maker, "although it may only be an accumulation of anguish, is dear to me, and I will defend it." And he adds, "I was benevolent and good; misery made me a fiend. Make me happy, and I shall again be virtuous."

The Monster offers Dr. Frankenstein a deal: that the doctor fashion a mate for him in his image, and both will disappear forever into the wilds of South America. (Note for South American readers: Poor Monster! Which of our countries will the Monster choose in search of a happy life? Pinochet's Chile? The generals' Argentina? Maduro's Venezuela? The Brazil of Bolsonaro?) Though Hollywood and director James Whale offered Elsa Lanchester and her rippling wig as the ideal spouse, in Shelley's version the doctor indignantly refuses the deal, and the Monster, after a long and painful flight through northern Europe, loses himself beyond the North Pole, in the frozen plains of Canada. Without Shelley's mentioning it, this final destination suits the Monster perfectly, since Canada is, in the world's imaginary geography, a vast blank page on which the dreams, hopes, and nightmares of humanity can be written.

James the Apostle, in his Universal Epistle (1:23–24),

compares he who attends to the divine word and does not act upon it to a man who sees himself in a mirror and then cannot remember who he is. "Because he considered himself, and went away; and then forgot what he was made of." A patch-up of so many men, Frankenstein's Monster is, at least in some part, our mirror, a reflection of that which we do not want to or do not dare remember. Perhaps that is why he frightens us.

SANDY

Road trips are among the best-loved of adventure stories, perhaps because they allow for unexpected branchings-off from the straight path to whatever goal is chosen. Dorothy and her friends on the road to Oz, the animal musicians of Bremen, Jack Kerouac and his buddies, the Three Musketeers, the wagon trailers in Louis L'Amour's westerns are some of the better-known travelers in the Western world. In China, however, without doubt the most popular and cherished adventurers of

the road are the three heroes who accompany a certain enlightened monk on his voyage to India in search of a collection of Buddhist scriptures (known in India as "Tripitaka," from which the monk takes his name). On the way, the three heroes defend Tripitaka from many-colored devils and evil monsters who believe they can become immortal by devouring Tripitaka's flesh. As Tripitaka reminds his friends to encourage them: "To save one life is better than to build a seven-storied pagoda." So many extraordinary things happen to the adventurers that the events stop being extraordinary, and the reader comes to expect another dragon, another celestial god, another magical beast to pop up on the next page. It always does.

The most famous of the three comrades who accompany Tripitaka (and the one who gives his name to Wu Cheng'en's novel in most Western versions) is Monkey, nicknamed "Aware-of-Vacuity" by the monk because of his awakening to the Truth. Monkey's birth was wondrous: he sprang to life on Flower-Fruit Mountain from a stone egg created by the coupling of Heaven and Earth (hence one of the titles by which the novel is known, *Story of the Stone;* another is *Journey to the West*). Monkey is a sort of trickster-hero whose goal is purely spiritual. When the Ten Judges of the Court of Death try to classify him, they find it is impossible: not being subject to the Unicorn, he does not fall into any animal category, and not being subject to the Phoenix, he cannot be classed as a bird. Finally, they find him under the heading "Soul 3150," a creature born as a "natural product" with a life-span of 342 years. This conclusion Monkey refuses to accept because all the while, says Wu Cheng'en of his hero, "his heart was set only on finding the Immortals and learning from them the secret of eternal youth." Monkey achieves this goal by eating the peaches of immortality.

Monkey is protected by several enchanted gifts: a gigantic staff of gold that he can shrink to the size of a needle and keep tucked in his ear, golden armor given to him by the Dragon King that fends off enemy weapons, and three jars of a magical elixir that cures all manner of ills. He is also able to fly, and can perform a remarkable "somersault cloud-leap" that allows him to travel many leagues in a single jump, like Puss-in-Boots. Together with Tripitaka, at the end of the journey Monkey achieves the much-desired Buddhahood.

With Monkey is Pigsy, whose Chinese name is Zhu Bajie, meaning "Swine-of-the-Eight-Prohibitions." Pigsy has the features of a nightmarish being, part human and part pig, a slothful glutton who is always lusting after beautiful women. These qualities create difficulties for preserving the spiritual nature of the journey, and earn for Pigsy the nickname Daizi, or "Moron." Before meeting Monkey, Pigsy was the commander-in-chief of eighty thousand soldiers in the Heavenly Navy, but he lost this exalted position because of his misdemeanors. The worst of these took place at a feast for the gods and goddesses in the Celestial Realm, during which Pigsy fell in love with the Moon Goddess and, in a drunken stupor, tried to seduce her. The goddess complained to the Jade Emperor and Pigsy was banished to Earth, where Monkey discovered and recruited him.

The third of the comrades, and the most mysterious, is Sandy. His real name is Sha-Wujing, meaning "Sand-

Awakened-to-Purity," and, like Pigsy, he was once a member of the Celestial Hosts, skilled in the arts of alchemy, in charge of lifting the curtain of the Imperial Chariot in the Hall of Miraculous Mist. His sin was less grievous than that of Pigsy, but equally deserving punishment according to celestial laws. He accidentally broke a glass beaker that belonged to the Queen Mother of the West during a Peach Banquet; for this, his features were changed into those of a monster, and he was, like Pigsy, exiled to Earth. Here he lived at the bottom of the Flowing Sands River (hence his nickname) from where he assaulted travelers attempting to cross to the other side. Monkey subdued the monster and convinced him to join Tripitaka's party.

Sandy's powers reside in a magical wooden rod decorated with strings of pearls, and in an ability to effect eighteen bodily changes that make him invincible in the water. Other than as a creature with vaguely frightening features, Sandy is ambiguously portrayed in the story. He is polite and considerate, reasonable and faithful to his masters, providing logical solutions to the problems the group encounters. "It has long been written in the *Book of Changes,* known as the *I Ching,* that mysteries have been elucidated and the prospects of the world made clear, so that people might know what to pursue and what avoid," says a prince they encounter on their way. This may be so, but it is Sandy who, discreetly and with great simplicity, helps his friends find their way.

Sandy is somewhat reminiscent of those steadfast helpers, the Tin Man of Oz and the Talking Cricket of Pinocchio, though the former receives for his efforts nothing more than a heart "made entirely of silk and stuffed with sawdust," and the latter is crushed against the wall by a hammer thrown by the moody puppet. Sandy, however, as a reward for his helpful efforts becomes an arhat at the end of the journey, one who has gained insight into the true nature of existence. He is thus ascended to a higher degree of enlightenment than that achieved by Pigsy, who is destined to sweep the altars of every Buddhist temple until the end of time.

Readers from the sixteenth century on have found entertainment in the madcap adventures of the three companions and their monk, but critics wanting to discover a different kind of quality in the story have sought to read it as an allegory of our path in the world like *Pilgrim's Progress* or as a quaint and primitive bildungsroman like *Tom Sawyer* or as a fierce satire of government bureaucracy like *The Trial*. The novel's first translator into English, Arthur Waley, pointed out that for the contemporaries of Wu Cheng'en, the hierarchy of heaven is a replica of the government on earth. "Heaven," wrote Waley, "is simply the whole bureaucratic system transferred bodily to the empyrean."

And yet, no reader today would see in Wu Cheng'en's adventure-filled world anything of the dark absurdity of Kafka's nightmares. If it is a satire of bureaucracy, it is an existential one that deems our existence subject to rules and regulations decreed from above, laws that we cannot understand but that we must nevertheless obey. Sandy's companions find pseudo-military strategies to ward off demons and gods and princes, but Sandy himself offers solutions in which a reasonable and ethical response becomes the best strategy for survival. It is not a moralistic consolation that he offers but a stern adherence to what is honestly right. In Sandy's conception of the world (as in that of Don Quixote) what seems just might in fact be a road to evil, and what seems evil might reveal itself as the right and proper way.

"He who does not believe that straight is straight must guard against the wickedness of good," says Sandy.

JONAH

Of all the snarling or moaning prophets who haunt the pages of the Old Testament, there is none so curious as the prophet known as Jonah. Ordinary people, we are told, were made nervous by his presence, and he acquired a posthumous reputation as a purveyor of bad luck. Perhaps the reason for this is that Jonah possessed what in the nineteenth century was called "an artistic temperament." Jonah was an artist.

The story of Jonah was probably written sometime in the fourth or fifth century B.C.E. The book of Jonah is

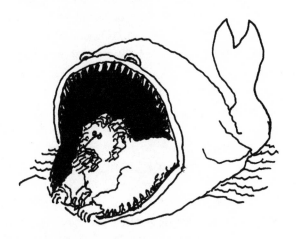

one of the shortest in the Bible—and one of the strangest. It tells how the prophet was summoned by God to go and cry against the city of Nineveh, whose wickedness had reached the ears of heaven. But Jonah refused because he knew that through his word the Ninevites would repent, and then God would forgive them, and they would escape the punishment they so dearly deserved. To avoid following the divine order, Jonah jumped on a ship sailing for the port of Tarshish. A furious storm arose, the sailors moaned in despair, and Jonah, somehow understanding that he was the cause of this meteorological turmoil, asked to be thrown into the sea to calm the waves. The sailors obliged, the storm died down, and Jonah was swallowed by a great fish, appointed for this purpose by God himself. There in the bowels of the creature, Jonah remained for three long days and nights. On the fourth day, God caused the fish to vomit the prophet out onto dry land and, once again, ordered Jonah to go to Nineveh and speak to the people. Resigned to God's will, this time Jonah obeyed. The king of Nineveh heard the warning and repented, and the city of Nineveh was saved.

But Jonah was furious with God and stormed out into the desert to the east of the city, where he set up a sort of booth, and sat and waited to see what would become of the repentant Nineveh. God then caused a plant to sprout up and protect Jonah from the sun. Jonah expressed his gratitude for the divine gift, but the next morning God caused the plant to wither. The sun and the wind beat hard on Jonah, and faint with heat he told God that it was better for him to die. Then God spoke to Jonah and said, "You are upset because I killed a simple plant and yet you wished me to destroy all the people of Nineveh. Should I have spared a plant but not spared these people who do not know their right hand from their left, and also much cattle?" With this unanswered question, the book of Jonah ends.

But what was the reason for Jonah's refusal to prophesy in Nineveh? The idea that Jonah would keep away from performing a divinely inspired piece because he knew his audience would repent and therefore be forgiven must seem incomprehensible to anyone except to an artist. As Jonah knew (though I believe this does not appear in his book), Ninevite society dealt in one of two ways with its artists: either it saw an accusation in an artist's work and blamed the artist for the evils of which society stood accused, or it assimilated the artist's work because, valued in dinars and nicely framed, art could serve as a pleasant decoration. In such circumstances, Jonah knew, no artist can win.

Given the choice between creating an accusation or a decoration, Jonah would probably have preferred the accusation. Like most artists, what Jonah really wanted was to stir the languid hearts of his listeners, to touch their sinews, to awaken in them something vaguely known yet utterly mysterious, to trouble their dreams and haunt their waking hours. What he certainly did not want, under any circumstances, was their repentance. Having the listeners simply say to themselves, "All's forgiven and forgotten, let's bury the past, let's not talk about injustice and the need for retribution, cuts in education and health programs, un-equal taxation and unemployment, and financial schemes that spell ruin for most; let exploiters shake hands with exploited, and on to our next glorious hour"—no, that was something Jonah certainly did not want. Nadine Gordimer, of whom Jonah had never heard, said that there could be no worse luck for a writer than *not* being execrated in a corrupt society. Jonah did not wish to suffer that annihilating fate.

Above all, Jonah was aware of the ongoing war in Nineveh between the politicians and the artists, a war in which Jonah felt that all the artists' efforts (beyond the efforts demanded by their craft) were ultimately futile because they took place in the political arena. It was a well-known fact that Ninevite artists, who had never tired in the pursuit of their vocation, grew quickly weary of the struggle with bureaucrats and banks, and the few heroes who continued the fight against royal clerks and money-lenders did so many times at the expense of both their art and their sanity. It was very difficult to go to one's studio or one's clay tablets after a day of committee meetings and official hearings. The bureaucrats of Nineveh counted on this, of course, and one of their most effective tactics was delay: delaying agreements, delaying the attribution of funds, delaying contracts, delaying appointments, delaying definitive answers. If they waited long enough, they said, the rage of the artist would fade or, rather, mysteriously turn into creative energy. The artist would go away and write a poem or do an installation or dream up a dance. And these things represented little danger to politicians and financial corporations. In fact, as business people well knew, many times this artistic rage became marketable merchandise. "Think," the Ninevites often said, "how much you'd pay today for the work of painters who in their time hardly had enough to buy paint, let alone food. Think of the protest songs by musicians who died in the poorhouse, sung today at national festivals under advertising banners. For an artist," they added knowingly, "posthumous fame is the best reward."

But the great coup of Ninevite politicians was getting artists to work against themselves. So imbued was Nineveh with the idea that wealth was the city's goal, and that art, since it was not an immediate producer of wealth, was an undeserving pursuit, that the artists themselves came to believe that they should pay for their own way in the world, producing cost-efficient art, frowning on failure, demanding positive discrimination and laws against voice appropriation, and, above all, trying to gratify those who, being wealthy, were also in positions of power. So visual artists were asked to make their work more pleasing, composers to write music with hummable tunes, writers to imagine not so depressing scenarios, and everyone to avoid producing something that anyone might consider disturbing or offensive.

In times long gone by, in short periods during which the bureaucrats slumbered, certain funds had been granted to artistic causes by soft-hearted or soft-headed Ninevite kings. Since those times, more conscientious officials had been redressing this financial oversight and vigorously pruning down the allotted sums. No official would, of course, recognize any such change in the government's support of the arts, and yet the Ninevite secretary of finance was able to cut the actual funds allotted to the arts down to almost nothing while at the same time advertising a committed increase of those same funds in the official records. This was done by the use of certain devices borrowed from the Ninevite poets (whose tools the politicians happily pilfered while despising the poets who invented them). Metonymy, for instance, the device by which a poet uses a part or an attribute of something to stand in its place (*crown* for *king,* for example), allowed the secretary of provisions to cut down on the funds spent on subsidizing artists' work materials. All any artist now received from the City, whatever his or her needs, was a number 4 rat-hair paintbrush, since in the secretary's official vocabulary "brush" was made to stand for "artist's equipment." Metaphors, the most common of poetic tools, were employed to great effect by these financial wizards. In one celebrated case, a sum of ten thousand gold dinars had been set aside long ago for the lodging of senior artists. By simply redefining camels, used in public transport, as "temporary lodgings," the secretary of finance was able to count the cost of the camels' upkeep (for which the City of Nineveh was responsible) as part of the sum allotted to artists' housing, since the senior artists did indeed use subsidized public camels to get from place to place.

"The real artists," said the Ninevites, "have no cause to complain. If they are really good at what they do, they will make a dinar no matter what the social conditions. It's the others, the so-called experimenters, the self-indulgers, the prophets, who don't make a cent and whine about their condition. A banker who doesn't know how to turn a profit would be lost. A bureaucrat who didn't recognize the need to clog things down would be out of a job. That is the law of survival. Nineveh is a society that looks to the future."

True, in Nineveh, a handful of artists (and many con artists) made a good living, and Ninevite society liked to reward a few of the makers of the products it consumed. What it would not recognize, of course, was the vast majority of the artists whose brave attempts and heroic failures allowed for the success of others. Ninevite society did not have to support anything it did not instantly like or understand. The truth was that this vast majority of artists would carry on, of course, no matter what, simply because they had to, the spirit urging them on night after night. They carried on writing and painting and composing and dancing by whatever means they could find. "Like every other worker in society," the Ninevites said.

It is told that the first time Jonah heard this particular point of Ninevite wisdom, he drummed up his prophetic courage and stood in the public square of Nineveh to address the crowds. "The artist," Jonah attempted to explain, "is not like every other worker in society. The artist deals with reality: inner and outer reality transformed into meaningful symbols. Those who deal in money deal in metaphors behind which stands nothing. It is wonderful to think of the thousands and thousands of Ninevite stockbrokers for whom reality is the arbitrary rising and falling of figures transformed in their dreams into wealth—a wealth that exists only in their imagination. No fantasy writer, no virtual-reality artist could ever aspire to create in an audience such an all-pervading trust in fiction as that which takes place in an assembly of stockbrokers.

Grownup men and women who will not for a minute consider the reality of the unicorn, even as a symbol, will accept as rock-hard fact that they possess a share in the nation's camel bellies, and in that belief they consider themselves happy and secure." By the time Jonah had reached the end of this paragraph, the public square of Nineveh was deserted.

For all these reasons, Jonah decided to escape both Nineveh and the Lord, and jumped on the ship headed for Tarshish. Now, the sailors in the ship that carried Jonah were all men from Joppa, a port not far from Nineveh. Nineveh was, as all knew, a society besotted by greed. Not ambition, which is a creative impulse, something all artists possess, but the sterile impulse to accumulate for the sake of accumulation. Joppa, however, had for many decades been a place where prophets had been allowed a tolerable amount of freedom. The people of Joppa accepted the yearly influx of bearded, ragged men and disheveled, wild-eyed women with a certain degree of sympathy since their presence procured Joppa free publicity when the prophets traveled abroad to other cities, where they often mentioned the name of Joppa in not unkind terms. Also, the recurrent prophesying season brought curious and illustrious visitors to Joppa, and neither the innkeepers nor the owners of the caravanserais complained of the demands made on their bed and board.

But when times were hard in Nineveh and the economic hardships of the city rippled out all the way to the little town of Joppa, when business profits were down and the wealthy Joppites were constrained to sell one of their ornamented six-horse chariots or close down a couple of their upland sweatshops, then the presence in Joppa of the prophesying artists was openly frowned upon. The tolerance and whimsical generosity of wealthier days seemed now sinfully wasteful to the citizens of Joppa, and many of them felt that the artists who came to their quaint little haven should make no demands and feel grateful for whatever they got: grateful when they were lodged in the frumpiest buildings of Joppa, grateful when they were denied appropriate work tools, grateful when they were allowed to finance on their own their crazy projects. When they were forced to move out of their rooms to accommodate paying guests from Babylon, the artists were told to remember that they, as artists, should know that it was an honorable thing to lie under the stars wrapped in smelly goat hides just like the illustrious prophets and poets of the days before the Flood.

And yet, even during those difficult times, most Joppites retained for the prophets a certain sincere fondness, somewhat akin to the affection one feels for old pets who have been around since childhood, and they tried in several ways to accommodate them even when the going was not good. Thus it was that when the storm rose and the ship from Joppa was tossed by furious waves, the Joppite sailors felt uneasy, and hesitated before blaming Jonah, their artistic guest. Unwilling to take any drastic measures, they tried praying to their own gods, whom they knew commanded the heavens and the sea, but with no visible results. In fact, the storm only got worse, as if the Joppite gods had other things to think about and were annoyed by the sailors' whining. Then the sailors appealed to Jonah (who was in the hold, sleeping out the storm, as artists sometimes do), and woke him and asked his advice. Even when Jonah told them, with a touch of artistic pride, that the storm was all his fault, the sailors felt reluctant to toss him overboard. How much of a gale could one scraggy artist raise? How angry could one miserable prophet make the wine-dark sea? But the storm grew worse, the wind howled through the rigging, the planks groaned and cried out when the waves hit them, and in the end, one by one, the sailors remembered the old Ninevite truisms learned at their grandmother's knee: all artists were, by and large, freeloaders, and the only thing Jonah and his ilk did all day was compose poems in which they kvetched about this and moaned about that, and said threatening things about the most innocent vices. And why should a society in which greed is the driving force support someone who does not contribute to the immediate accumulation of wealth? Therefore, as one of the sailors explained to his mates, don't blame yourselves for bad seamanship. Simply accept Jonah's mea culpa and throw the bastard into the water. He won't resist. In fact, he asked for it.

Now, even if Jonah had had second thoughts, and had argued that perhaps a ship, or a ship of state, could in fact do with a few wise prophecies to serve as ballast and keep it steady, the sailors had learned from long familiarity with Ninevite politicians the craft of turning a deaf ear. Zig-zagging their way across the oceans of the world in search of new lands on which to conduct free and profitable trade, the sailors assumed that whatever an artist might say or do, the weight of money would always provide a steadier ballast than any artistic argument.

When they threw Jonah overboard and the sea became calm again, the sailors fell on their knees and thanked the God of Jonah. No one enjoys being tossed about in a rocking ship, and since the rocking had stopped as soon as Jonah hit the water, the sailors immediately concluded that he was indeed to blame and that their action had been justified. These sailors had obviously not had the benefit of a classical education or the gift of foresight, or they would have known that the argument for the elimination of the artist had once enjoyed (and was again to acquire in the coming centuries) a venerable reputation. They would have known that there is an ancient impulse, running through the foundations of every human society, to shun the uncomfortable creature who keeps attempting to shift the tenets of our certitudes. For Plato, to begin with, the real artist is the statesman, the person who shapes the state according to a divine model of Justice and Beauty. The ordinary artist, on the other hand, the writer or the painter, does not reflect this worthy reality but produces instead mere fantasies, which are unfit for the education of the young.

This notion, that art is only useful if it serves the state, was heartily embraced by successions of diverse governments: Emperor Augustus banished the poet Ovid because of something the poet had written which Augustus felt was secretly threatening. The church condemned artists who distracted the faithful from the sacred dogma. In the Renaissance, artists were bought and sold like courtesans, and in the eighteenth and nineteenth centuries they were reduced (at least in the public imagination) to garret-living creatures dying of melancholy and consumption.

Flaubert penned the bourgeois view of the artist in his *Dictionary of Clichés:* "Artists: All clowns. Praise their self-lessness. Be astonished at the fact they dress like everyone else. They earn fabulous sums but they squander every last cent. Often invited to dinner at the best houses. All female artists are sluts."

So Jonah was thrown into the water and swallowed by a big fish. Life in the dark soft belly of the fish was actually not that bad. During those three days and nights, lulled by the rumblings of ill-digested plankton and shrimp, Jonah had time to reflect. This was a luxury artists seldom have. In the belly of the fish were no deadlines, no grocer's bills to pay, no diapers to wash, no dinners to cook, no family conflicts to be dragged into just as the right word comes to complete the sonnet, no bank managers to plead with, no critics to gnash teeth over. So during those three days and three nights Jonah thought and prayed and slept and dreamed. And when he woke up, he found himself vomited onto dry land and the nagging Voice of God was at him again: "Go on, go seek out Nineveh and do your bit. It doesn't matter how they react. Every artist needs an audience. You owe it to your work."

This time Jonah did as God told him. Some degree of confidence in the importance of his craft had come to him in the fish's dark belly, and he felt moved to put his art on display in Nineveh. But barely had he begun his performance, barely had he said five words of his prophetic text, when the king of Nineveh fell on his knees and repented, the people of Nineveh ripped open their shirts and repented, and even the cattle of Nineveh bellowed out in unison to show that they too, repented. And the king, the people, and the cattle of Nineveh all dressed in sackcloth and sprinkled their heads with ashes, and assured one another that bygones were bygones, and wailed their repentance to the Lord above. And seeing this orgiastic display of repentance, God withdrew his threat from the people and cattle of Nineveh. And Jonah, of course, was furious. What some have called the "anarchic" spirit rebelled inside Jonah, and he went off to sulk in the desert at some distance from the forgiven city.

We must remember that God caused a plant to grow from the bare soil to shade Jonah from the heat, and that this charitable gesture of God's made Jonah once again thankful, after which God withered the plant back into the dust and Jonah found himself roasting in the sun for a second time. We do not know whether God's trick with the plant was a lesson meant to convince Jonah of his good intentions. Perhaps Jonah saw in the gesture an allegory of the funds first given to him and then withdrawn after the cuts by the Nineveh National Endowment for the Arts—a gesture that left him to fry unprotected in the midday sun. Jonah no doubt understood that in times of difficulty—in times when the poor are poorer and the rich can barely keep in the zillion-dollar tax bracket— God was not going to concern himself with questions of artistic merit. Being an author himself, God had no doubt some sympathy with Jonah's predicament: wanting time to work on his thoughts without having to think about his bread and butter; wanting his prophecies to appear on the *Nineveh Times* best-seller list and yet not wanting to be confused with the authors of pot-boilers and tearjerkers;

wanting to stir the crowds with his searing words, but to stir them into revolt, not into compliance; wanting Nineveh to look deep into its soul and recognize that its strength, its wisdom, its very life lay not in the piles of coins growing daily like funeral pyramids on the financiers' desks but in the work of its artists and the words of its poets, and in the visionary rage of its prophets, whose job it was to keep the boat rocking in order to keep the citizens awake. All this God understood, as he understood Jonah's anger, because it is not impossible to imagine that God himself sometimes learns something from his artists.

However, though God could draw water from a stone and cause the people of Nineveh to repent, he still could not make them think. The cattle, incapable of thought, he could pity. But speaking to Jonah as Creator to creator, as Artist to artist, what was God to do with a people who, as he said with such divine irony, "don't know their right hand from their left"?

At this, Jonah nodded, and was silent.

DOÑA EMILIA

Perhaps countries might be defined through the best-loved characters in their children's books. England would be seen as Alice, constantly confronted by absurd social rules and prejudices, Italy as the rebellious and fun-loving Pinocchio, who wants to become "a real boy," Switzerland as the goody-goody Heidi, Canada as the intelligent and concerned survivalist Anne of Green Gables. Perhaps the United States would see itself reflected in Dorothy, the heroine who must in the end

discover that the Emerald City owes its wonderful color to the green-tinted glasses its citizens are forced to wear, and that the governing Wizard is nothing but a fraud whose success lies in giving people what they think they want, in brief emotional outbursts. "How can I help being a humbug," the great Oz asks in the last pages of the story, "when all these people make me do things that everybody knows can't be done?"

In this context, Brazil might be seen as Dona Emilia, the patchwork doll made out of bits and pieces of different cloths, brought to life by the black cook Aunt Anastasia on the Yellow Woodpecker Ranch, somewhere in the Brazilian farmland. Outside Brazil, and to a certain extent in a few other South American countries, Dona Emilia and Aunt Anastasia and the rest of the inhabitants of the ranch are unknown, but in Brazil they are immortal, thanks to the books by the early-twentieth-century writer José Bento Renato Monteiro Lobato.

The Yellow Woodpecker Ranch is the property of Dona Benta and her two grandchildren, Pedrinho and Lucia, the latter known as Narizinho because of her small, turned-up nose. On the farm, the children and their grandmother bring to life a host of imaginary (and not so imaginary) characters that includes the wise corncob puppet called the Viscount of Sabugosa, the one-legged Saci Perere and his foul-smelling pipe, and a variety of talking animals. There's also a frightening bogey creature, Cuca, who comes at night to trouble the children's dreams.

Dona Emilia is Narizinho's favorite and she will refuse to take a meal unless Dona Emilia is seated next to her. Thanks to a pill given to the doll by the mysterious

Doctor Caramujo, Dona Emilia can talk. Her first words are a complaint about the horrid taste of toad skin that the pill left in her mouth, and from then on, Dona Emilia becomes a fount of critical observations, ironic bon mots, anarchic ideas, and independent thoughts that create a bubbling verbal universe often more powerful and true than that of the world of pampas grass and palm trees.

A few volumes into the saga, Dona Emilia decides to write her memoirs, imitating those of another illustrious builder of worlds, "the Englishman Robinson Crusoe." Her memoirs begin in the traditional style: "I was born in the year *** in the city of *** of a poor but honest family." When the Viscount, who in spite of being the most learned is duped into becoming her scribe, asks her whether all the asterisks are meant to hide her real age, Dona Emilia, eternal troublemaker, answers, "No. That is merely to bother future meddlesome historians." Asked by Dona Benta to explain what are these memoirs she is writing, Dona Emilia explains, "A writer of memoirs writes until he feels that the day of his death approaches. Then he stops and leaves the ending blank. And then dies in peace." And she adds, "But I don't intend to die. I'll just pretend I'm dying and my last words will be: 'Then I died.'" Tristram Shandy remembering the days before his birth and Dona Emilia those after her death stand at the two literary poles of the craft of autobiography.

Dona Emilia has magical powers and can travel through time and space, sometimes taking Narizinho and Pedrinho with her to distant planets and ages past. She leaves her mark wherever she goes and introduces the children to all sorts of fantastic creatures and historical figures, whether a centaur, a Hercules, or a Pericles. Asked whether she tells the truth in all these adventures, Dona Emilia explains, "The truth is a sort of lie well stitched-together, a lie that no one doubts. Just that."

After Monteiro Lobato's death, critics accused him of racism and attempted to ban his work (as in England they attempted to ban the Noddy books of Enid Blyton and in Japan the adventures of Pinocchio), pointing out demeaning references to the black characters in his stories. Those claims may be true of the author, but they miss what children read in these stories, and what as adults they remember. Something in the adventures at the Yellow Woodpecker Ranch rises far above whatever prejudices their author might have privately held and transforms Dona Emilia and her friends into trustworthy, even necessary companions in our path through the well stitched-together lies that have become our map of the world.

THE WENDIGO

We have long known that everything must have its shadow: day has night, conscious life sleep, public face hidden private thoughts. At one of the doors of a small church in northern Quebec is the statue of a woman: if seen from the front, her appearance is comely, but from the back she reveals a mass of worms and maggots crawling through the exposed innards and ribs.

Alone in the wintry regions of Canada that stretch from the Saint-Maurice to the Ottawa rivers, the Algon-

quian hunters dreamed up a terrible companion that would lend a shape to their fears. The howling wind gave it swiftness and voice, the snow a heart of ice, the tall trees a gigantic stature, the torn mist its mutilated face and gnawed lips through which the teeth menacingly appear. But more hideous than this, the hunters' own dread of starvation gave the creature a lust for human flesh.

They called it the Wendigo, or Windigo, or Wittako, or Wittikka (there are thirty-eight different spellings), and in the tongue of other tribes it took on other names, such as Atchen or Wechuge. In 1743, the trader James Isham noted the word as "Whiteco" and translated it bluntly as "The Devil." At the beginning, those who believed in the Wendigo attempted in numerous chronicles to confess to a heart-gripping terror which they were unable to put into words. In later accounts, only the ghost of this ghostly fear remains, and the Wendigo is either inspected with anthropological cold-bloodedness or psychological curiosity, or rebuilt from its icy skeleton with the tools of fiction, as in some of the stories of Algernon Blackwood and August Derleth.

Like the vampire or the werewolf, the Wendigo is a contagious spirit and can make wendigos of us all. John Robert Colombo, Wendigo connoisseur, explains the several ways in which this may come to pass: "Being bitten by the creature is certain contamination. To dream of a Wendigo is to become a Wendigo. A medicine man or shaman through his sorcery may metamorphose a healthy person into a blood-thirsty monster overnight." Once infected, death is the only escape for the unfortunate victim. In David Thompson's story "Man Eaters," we read about a certain Nahathaway, or Cree Indian, "a good Beaver worker and trapper, but an indifferent Moose Hunter," who "had been twice so reduced by hunger as to be twice on the point of eating one of his children." This Saturnine urge remained with him and got worse when he drank grog. He would then mutter in a thoughtful manner "Nee weet to go" (which Thompson helpfully translates for us as "I must be a man-eater"), at which point his companions would tie him up until he became quiet. Thompson concludes: "Three years afterward, this sad mood came upon him so often that the Natives got alarmed. They shot him, and burnt his body to ashes, to prevent his ghost remaining in this world."

Hunger breeds hunger, and particularly prone to the Wendigo's attention are greedy eaters. Diamond Jenness, an anthropologist, states that "a glutton who eats butter or fat by spoonfuls, or drinks gravy from a bowl instead of mixing it with his potatoes, is especially liable to develop into a Wendigo. Children are, therefore, trained to eat carefully."

The Wendigo, as stated, is a cannibal but also, more mysteriously, a nightmare image of ourselves, a double like the German doppelgänger and Scottish fetch (which "fetches" those about to die). To meet one's double is a sign of imminent misfortune (except in Jewish folklore, where the meeting anticipates the gift of prophecy), and the victim is ostracized by his or her fellows. This aspect of the Wendigo is described in a ballad by C. D. Shanly, "The Walker of the Snow," published in May 1859, in which a lost traveler meets a "dusky figure" who, Virgil-like, walks by his side but leaves "no foot-marks on the snow." The apparition is so frightening that the traveler's hair turns white, and when he is rescued by a party of otter trappers, no one dares speak to him. "But they spoke not as they raised me / For they knew that in the night / I had seen the shadow hunter / And had withered in his blight."

Is it the whiteness of the frozen spaces of the North that require the ghostly presence of the Wendigo, or is it the nightmarish figure that, too terrible to accept as our mind's creation, we anchor in the blank page of the winter landscape? The Arabian desert breeds the *fata morgana,* the green hills of Ireland are riddled with Little Men, the fathomless ocean is home to the Kraken, which will rise only once the final trumpet has sounded. Canada has chosen to be haunted by something as vast and white as its image in the classroom atlas, undefined and secret, the terrible shadow of its welcoming self.

HEIDI'S GRANDFATHER

Nobody seems to know much about this hermit's life.
He is supposed to be nasty, grumpy, and unsociable, with
a reputation for showing people the door if they come
up to his cottage high in the Swiss Alps. From one year's
end to the other he keeps away from church. People think
him a heathen, with his shaggy eyebrows that meet in the
middle like a thicket and his huge, disheveled gray beard.
When once every twelve months he wanders along the
mountain road with his twisted stick, people keep out of

his way. Everyone is afraid of meeting him alone. They call him the Alm-Uncle (Mountain-Uncle), but no one knows exactly why.

Rumor has it that the Alm-Uncle was once heir to a large farm in a neighboring town and that in his youth, playing the fine gentleman, he lost everything to drink and gambling. His Calvinist parents died of grief, and he himself disappeared for a time, no one knows exactly where. After many years he returned to the village with a half-grown son, Tobias. Tobias became a carpenter and turned out to be a quiet, steady fellow, eventually marrying a girl called Adelheid. One day, when Tobias was helping to build a house, a beam fell on him and killed him. Adelheid never recovered from the shock and only a few weeks after Tobias's death she too died, leaving behind a one-year-old baby girl, called Heidi after her mother. People said that the heavens had punished the Alm-Uncle for his misdeeds, and the fact is that after the death of his son, he never spoke to a living soul. He moved up into the Alps and lived there from then on, "sans teeth, sans eyes, sans taste, sans everything," as Hamlet would have it, cursing God and all his works.

Heidi is brought up by her maternal aunt and her daughter, but when the daughter is offered a job in Frankfurt, they decide to leave Heidi with her misanthropic grandfather. This suits Heidi perfectly. In the old man's cottage with the goats (the white one is called Schwänli and the brown one Bärli), sleeping on a bed of hay that she has chosen for herself, surrounded by a picture-postcard landscape of white flowers and screeching eagles, the five-year-old Heidi finds that she is free to do as she likes.

And even later, when she is sent to Frankfurt to be educated in the manners of civilized folk and becomes the companion of an invalid child, she continues to exercise her freedom, finding ways to help the people she has left behind, even though, as she later tells her grandfather, she sometimes felt she couldn't bear to be away from him and the mountains, and thought she would choke because she could not tell anyone about her sorrow, "for that would have been ungrateful." A wild child (like Huckleberry Finn, like Mowgli, like Peter Pan), Heidi has the nature of Rousseau's *bon sauvage,* intrinsically good, bringing soft rolls from the city for the toothless blind old woman she befriends, and caring for all. The world sees in Heidi the emblem of the Swiss, offering the equivalent of comforting chocolates and offshore accounts.

In the end, the old heathen is saved. "Nobody can come back to the Lord, when God has once forgotten him," he says to Heidi, and she corrects this dogmatic error. "But grandfather," she tells him, "everybody can come back to Him." Convinced by Heidi, the grandfather attends church for the first time since the death of his son and experiences a spiritual rebirth. "You see," he says to Heidi, "I'm more happy than I deserve; to be at peace with God and men makes one's heart feel light. God has been good to me, to send you back." We can almost hear the church bells pealing in the background and the angelic choirs up on high. This is a highly suspicious ending for the autarchic old goat, who always seems about to explode behind his stern, disheveled features.

If Heidi is an outgoing, redeeming figure, who is the gruff, at-length-redeemed grandfather? What does he

stand for, tucked in upon himself like a porcupine, in his
bucolic domain close to the skies?

Neutral, diminutive, mountain-enclosed Switzerland
is said to defend itself on the Porcupine Principle: roll up
into a ball and brandish your quills. For seven centuries,
the Swiss have been of the opinion that the best defense
is not to attack but to be quietly armed up to their yo-
deling teeth. They have never engaged in a battle abroad,
even when the world wars raged around them. Their
army is made up of their citizens, who have the obligation to train, and who keep their uniforms and weapons
at home, next to their alpenstocks and lederhosen. They
have turned their country into a massive explosives dump,
wiring all strategic tunnels and bridges to be blown up
in case of invasion, at the flick of a preventive finger.
Sabotage, for the enemies of Switzerland, would mean
removing, not placing, bombs. The unofficial motto of
Switzerland is, not without a certain irony, that of the
Three Musketeers: "All for One and One for All."

John Ruskin abominated what he called "the pathetic
fallacy," the attribution of human emotions to a landscape,
and argued that "the man who perceives rightly in spite
of his feelings" will see the things of this world, like a
primrose, "in the very plain and leafy fact of it, whatever
and how many soever the associations and passions may
be that crowd around it." And yet: is it a mistake to see
the mountain man who is Heidi's unwilling grandfather
echoed in the mountainous country in which he lives,
deceptively going about his own business but all the time
harboring in his depths explosive passions and warning,
"Trespassers Will Be Shot"?

CLEVER ELSIE

Fairy tales have a way of surreptitiously explaining much of what is dark and frightening in our world. Our skeptical nature has lent them the connotation of falsehoods, wishful and illusory, but something deeper than incredulity will not allow us to forget that the remedy to a curse may be a hundred years' sleep and that something vicious and toothy may be lying expectantly in our granny's bed.

"Clever Elsie" tells the story of a girl promised by her

parents to be married if she proves to be not only clever but also careful. During the meal to which her parents have invited Hans, her husband-to-be, Elsie goes down into the cellar to draw some beer. Looking up at the ceiling, she notices a pickax stuck to the beam just above her head and thinks, "If I marry and have a child, and it grows up, and I send him into the cellar to draw beer, that pickax might fall on his head and kill him!" Panic-stricken, Elsie bursts into tears. In the meantime, her parents, worried because Elsie is taking so long to return to the table, send the maid down to see what has happened. Elsie explains to the maid the cause of her fears and the maid joins her mistress in the weeping and wailing. A servant boy is then sent down to enquire about the maid, the mother follows the boy, the father follows the mother, and they all lament most pitifully the fate of the son who might one day be born. Last, Hans joins the family in the cellar, hears their story, and tells them that Elsie is indeed "clever and careful" and that the marriage should go ahead. The question of the beer is entirely forgotten.

We all have been, at some point, called into the cellar to bear witness to something supposedly imminent and to bemoan a tragedy that has not yet taken place, rather than remove the pickax that might one day threaten the life of a nonexistent child. There is a difference between serious concerns about the state of things caused by corruption and greed and the thirst for violence, and the fabricated feeling of impending doom for which no one is held responsible. Terrible things have indeed happened and are still happening every day and every night but not because

of a pickax that might one afternoon fall and kill us—
rather, because of the deeds of a number of amoral men
and women. "The gods have become diseases," wrote
C. G. Jung ten years after the end of World War II. "Zeus
no longer rules Olympus but rather the solar plexus and
produces curious specimens for the doctor's consulting
room, or disorders the brains of politicians and journalists
who unwittingly let loose psychic epidemics on the world."

Daily panic provoked by charges of "fake news" and
conspiracy theories has been extremely useful for those
in power because fear allows them to take measures and
issue decrees that would never be allowed to pass in more
reasonable times. "Why did no political economist fore-
see this coming?" is the question the Elsies ask when the
dark clouds of doom are announced on the evening news,
and they demand that our political economists issue force-
ful proclamations of wishful thinking. "The real science
of political economy," wrote John Ruskin in *Unto This
Last,* "which has yet to be distinguished from the bastard
science, as medicine from witchcraft, and astronomy from
astrology, is that which teaches nations to desire and labor
for the things that lead to life: and which teaches them
to scorn and destroy the things that lead to destruction."
Confronted with falsehoods, the motto of gullible readers
is that of Saint Paul: "I believe because it's impossible"; the
motto of fiction readers that of the Mock Turtle: "Well, I
never heard it before, but it sounds uncommon nonsense."

What will happen if, like Elsie, we persist in such
so-called cleverness? What will happen if we give up sane
reflection and allow ourselves to be drawn into a brain-
washing state of panic, reacting to incoherent political

blurtings and conspiracy theories, no longer able to act as reflecting individuals, no longer knowing who we really are?

The fairy tale offers a cautionary ending. After marrying Elsie, Hans sends her into the field to work. But Clever Elsie decides first to eat and then to nap, so when her husband comes to fetch her home, he finds her fast asleep in the midst of the uncut corn. To punish her, he covers her with a bird-net decked with little bells and leaves her to her slumbers. When Elsie wakes, she sees that it has grown dark, she hears the bells tinkling, and she begins to wonder whether she is really herself. Bewildered. she returns to her house and knocks on the window. "Is Elsie home?" she calls out. "Yes," answers her ruthless husband. "She is here." Then a great panic comes over Elsie. "O dear, so I am not I," she cries, and runs away, stripped of her name and her person, far beyond her village. And no one has seen her since.

LONG JOHN SILVER

The story of the birth of *Treasure Island* is well known; that of its most famous pirate, less so. Robert Louis Stevenson and his family had returned to England in July 1880 after an exhausting sojourn in California, and his parents, worried by his poor health, suggested a rest cure in Braemar, Scotland. Stevenson and his thirteen-year-old stepson, Lloyd Osborne, had begun a literary collaboration sometime earlier. Stevenson had given the boy as a present a miniature printing press, and obeying the urgent

requests of the brand-new publisher he composed a series of poetic "emblems" that were printed, with woodcuts by the author, in a small edition limited to the family.

In Braemar, Lloyd decorated his room with drawings he had made himself, and Stevenson offered to contribute to the decorations a hand-colored map of an imaginary island. Bending to the insistence of Lloyd, who rightly supposed that behind the map lay a story, Stevenson began telling a tale of pirates and buried treasure. The only demand made by Stevenson's singular audience was there were to be no women in the plot. The story began to flow with such ease that Stevenson decided to put it in writing. Every evening, after the work of the day had been completed, Stevenson would read out loud to Lloyd what he had written. Soon, to the audience of one was added Stevenson's father, and both the old man and the young boy followed with rapt enthusiasm the unfolding adventures. Stevenson's writing until then had consisted of short stories, poems, and essays. He had never attempted a novel. Now the opportunity had presented itself as if by magic.

Throughout his life, Stevenson had been plagued by tuberculosis, and after finishing chapter 16 he felt too weak to continue. But when a children's magazine, *Young Folk,* offered to publish the work in installments under the title *The Sea Cook,* he knew he had to find a way of carrying on. Stevenson was thirty-one at the time, the only breadwinner in the family.

To enable Stevenson to breathe better air, the family traveled to Davos, in Switzerland. There he felt invigorated and capable of returning to work. Sitting in bed, since he was forbidden to rise until midday so as not to overstrain his lungs, he wrote chapter after chapter, and in the evenings he used his newfound strength to read them out loud to his family. After the last chapter was published in the magazine, Stevenson decided to change the title and call the book *Treasure Island*.

Several of the characters are memorable: Captain Billy Bones, singing his pirate song and waiting patiently for a death foreseen; the abominable Blind Pew, whose voice is more violent than his violent gestures; decent Squire Trelawney, who puts his trust too readily in appearances; stern Dr. Livesey, seduced by hidden treasure; the abandoned Ben Gunn, trapped on the island, this side of madness; the narrator, young Jim Hawkins, who risks his life and that of his companions for the thrill of an adventure. But none is as memorable as Long John Silver, the one-legged mariner, whose parrot repeats the ominous words "Pieces of eight!" When, a third through the book, Silver is recruited as the ship's cook by the artless Trelawney, both the squire and the doctor call Silver "an honest man," associating his character with a name that universally stands for steadfastness and purity. The adjective *honest* will echo through the book as a sardonic warning to the reader.

Silver is shady, undefined, clever, intimately ambiguous. In order to bring him to life, Stevenson thought of his friend William Ernest Henley. Henley was a man of letters, a better reader than writer, who had suffered in his childhood from tubercular arthritis, an illness that caused him to have one of his feet amputated. During his convalescence in the hospital, Henley met Stevenson, and the

two men became great friends, collaborating in a few de-
servedly forgotten plays. If as a writer he was not distinguished, as an editor he was intelligent and risk taking, and
he was one of the first to publish the works of Kipling,
Henry James, and H. G. Wells. Stevenson, writing to
Henley in 1883, confessed to his friend that "it was the
sight of your maimed strength and masterfulness that
begot Long John Silver . . . the idea of the maimed man,
ruling and dreaded by the sound, was entirely taken from
you." And yet, there was perhaps more to the portrait of
the buccaneer and sea cook. Henley's ambiguous personality, his intellectual strength, his diminished physical
appearance, his extravagant manners, and his boundless
ambition found their dark mirror in the character of the
pirate.

Two scenes define Long John Silver: the first the
murder of Tom the sailor, the second the deal that Silver
proposes to the boy Jim. When the mutiny is announced,
faithful Tom addresses Silver with these wishful words:
"Silver, you're old, and you're honest, or has the name for
it; and you've money too, which lots of poor sailors hasn't;
and you're brave, or I'm mistook. And will you tell me
you'll let yourself be led away with that kind of a mess of
swabs? Not you!" Later, realizing his mistake and becoming aware that Silver is himself one of the mutineers, Tom
tries to escape, but he is struck by a branch thrown at him
by Silver with the help of his crutch. (This scene was
perhaps inspired by a story Stevenson might have heard
about Oscar Wilde and Stevenson's friend Henley. The two
men were hotly arguing about something after leaving a
theater in London. When they parted, Wilde turned to

make one final remark, and Henley hurled his crutch at Wilde's head.) After Silver throws the branch at Tom, Tom falls, and Silver knifes him to death. Atrociously, Stevenson make us see that nothing in the world will change after this crime has been committed, one of the many of which Silver is guilty in his violent long life. Jim, witness of the horror, can barely believe that the sun keeps on calmly shining after a human life has been taken in this particularly vicious way.

In the second scene, Jim is no longer a witness but the protagonist. The deal that Silver proposes to him is that they protect one another: the buccaneer will defend Jim against the mutineers, and the boy will defend Silver later, in front of the judge, to save him from the gallows. And Silver says to Jim, "Ah, you that's young—you and me might have done a power of good together!" The temptation of a pirate's life is made explicit. Over Silver's words falls the shadow of what might have been, and the boy discovers the tenuous border between a civilized behavior that obeys society's laws and the life of an adventurer that follows the call of blood.

In the final moments, Jim remains faithful to the old buccaneer, keeps his side of the bargain, and will not abandon Silver even though Dr. Livesey insists he do so. Without the reader ever discovering precisely how, Silver has turned the muddled boy into an "honest" young man. As Captain Smollett says to Squire Trelawney when he shrouds the body of one his faithful followers with a British flag, "It mayn't be good divinity, but it's a fact."

The adventure, as is literarily appropriate, ends with Silver, "sitting back almost out of the firelight, but eating heartily, prompt to spring forward when anything was wanted, even joining quietly in our laughter—the same bland, polite, obsequious seaman of the voyage out." When, on the last page, Jim tells the reader what happened afterwards to each of the main characters, he says that he has had no news from Silver himself, but that he imagines the buccaneer has met his old black mistress, and perhaps still lives in peace with her and his parrot. "It is to be hoped so, I suppose," says Jim, "for his chances of comfort in another world are very small." The reader feels an uneasy affection for the infamous pirate who was a traitor, a thief, a murderer, and also a good and honest man.

KARAGÖZ AND HACIVAT

There are characters conceived in pairs—Don Quixote and Sancho Panza, Sherlock Holmes and Watson—who can, however, exist, do exist, individually. In his first adventures Don Quixote is bravely alone; in some of his early and later cases, Sherlock Holmes detects without the dubious assistance of his faithful doctor friend. Other couples, however, have never been seen apart. Castor and Pollux (brothers of the beautiful Helen and the murderous Clytemnestra), Wilhelm Busch's naughty Max and

Moritz, Hansel and Gretel, Tweedledee and Tweedledum come to life only as two. And among this indivisible category, we find the Turkish version of Punch and Judy: the *frères ennemis* Karagöz and Hacivat.

According to one legend, Karagöz and Hacivat were born out of a poor peasant's attempt to present his plight to the mighty sultan. Like Hamlet, the peasant decided to show rather than tell, and had a couple of shadow puppets cut out of camel hide perform the tale of how the corrupt and recognizable court officials had swindled him. The sultan was so pleased with the show that he appointed the peasant grand vizier and severely punished the accused officials. In another version of their birth, Karagöz and Hacivat are said to be masons working on the erection of a mosque in Bursa who willfully distracted their fellow workers with their tricks so that the completion of mosque was endlessly delayed. The angry sultan ordered their execution; as a tribute to their clowning, the fatal buffoons were immortalized as shadows on the puppet stage.

Certain scholars have seen in the character of Karagöz the incarnation of the human body from the waist down—eating, farting, and making love—while in that of Hacivat, that of the body from the waist up—the clever brain and the temperamental heart. Like the two parts of one body, Karagöz and Hacivat are complementary. In fact, they stand at opposite ends of the social spectrum. Karagöz (his name means "black-eyed") is, like Sancho, an illiterate man of the people, witty and straightforward in his opinions. Hacivat instead is cultured, discreet, well-mannered, sneaky, and egotistical, always full of get-rich-quick plans that are obviously doomed to failure. Hacivat speaks Ottoman Turkish, can quote classical poetry, and tries to civilize Karagöz, as Don Quixote does with Sancho. And like the earnest knight, Hacivat never succeeds.

Opposing characters appear early in our stories. In the Epic of Gilgamesh, composed over four millennia ago, the tyrannical king Gilgamesh learns from the wild man Enkidu to be aware of the needs of his suffering subjects and becomes a better ruler, while Enkidu, after spending seven nights with the temple prostitute Shamhat, is introduced to the trappings and conventions of Gilgamesh's civilization, thereby losing much of his primal knowledge of the natural world. In the exchange, the two men become lovers. This is not the case of Karagöz and Hacivat, except that they too exist in the tension between both of their own worlds: the old and the new, the carnal and the intellectual, the living flesh and the inventive spirit.

Hacivat and Karagöz are accompanied by a host of eccentric characters that cover all the multicultural Turkish society and serve to bounce off the couple's idiosyncrasies: Denyo the dullard, the kind-hearted Efe from Aydin, who protects the weak against bullies, an opium addict called Tiryaki, Alti Karis Beberuhi the dwarf, the drunkard Tuzsuz Deli Bekir, the penny-pinching Civan, and the nymphomaniac Kanli Nigar, as well as a number of nameless characters, such as the Arab beggar who speaks no Turkish, a black maid, a Circassian servant girl, an insolent Albanian watchman, a Greek doctor, an Armenian banker, a Jewish jeweler, and a Persian who recites poetry with an Azerbaijani accent. The whole of the Middle East parades across their stage.

The adventures of Karagöz and Hacivat follow a traditional pattern. Each one begins with a "mukaddime," or prologue, in which Hacivat sings a song to the sound of a tambourine, recites a short prayer, and then explains to the audience that he is looking for his friend Karagöz. The two men meet, they argue, they fight, and in the end, neither of them wins. In the final scene of each adventure, Hacivat accuses Karagöz of having ruined the story, to which a seemingly contrite Karagöz replies, "May my transgressions be forgiven." There is something pleasingly true in this recurrent ending: their relationship doesn't admit of resolution. As fabulous creatures, their bickering will last throughout eternity. Nietzsche, who believed that we are all predestined to repeat the same events over and over again, would have approved. For Albert Camus, this repetition mirrored the absurdity of life, but he argued that it also lent a sort of resigned contentment to our endeavors. In that case, and in spite of all their failures, Hacivat and Karagöz must be happy.

Do Turkish people see in the eternal misadventures of the pair a mirror of their own history, one half seeking to civilize the other half, one constantly in pursuit of the new, the other determinedly gripping on to the traditions of their remotest ancestors from long before the Ottomans? "History is a bridge," said Atatürk, the father of modern Turkey, in a 1933 speech. "We must delve into our roots and reconstruct what history has divided. We can't wait for them to approach us. We must reach out to them."

As for the history of Karagöz and Hacivat, and for whatever noble or selfish reasons, Hacivat reaches out to Karagöz over and over again, always unsuccessfully. Whether Karagöz wants to be reached is a different question. In the meantime, their adventures continue.

ÉMILE

Rousseau wrote *Émile* in 1762, the year in which he
published *The Social Contract.* One could call the book
a sort of *Social Contract* for children: replace *man* with
child in the first line of the *Contract,* and you have *Émile*
summed up for you: "The child is born free and every-
where he is in chains." It is a curious hodgepodge of a
book, half novel and half sermon. André Gide thought it
unreadable. But for certain more patient readers it merits
consideration, if nothing else, because instead of merely

criticizing our systems of education it proposes a new one: not universal but particular to each child.

Rousseau lays out Émile's education plan in five stages. Stage One is separating the child from society so that its "good nature" might grow unimpeded; Two, allowing its senses to enjoy the world without punishment or censure of any kind; Three, enjoining it to learn pragmatically, from material experience; Four, permitting it to develop its relationships with others in the fields of sex, social manners, religion, and morals; and finally, Five, introducing it to a life partner (in Émile's case, the goody-goody Sophie), so that it can become a parent and educate its own child in turn. Rousseau addressed the book to "a good mother who knows how to think." Perhaps he was foreseeing D. W. Winnicott's notion of the "good enough" parent.

A number of generations have passed since Émile became a father and Sophie a mother. Several millions of new Émiles busy themselves in a world in which things have much changed, not least our vision of childhood. No longer believed to be intrinsically good just because he is a child, little Émile is not for that reason any more an individual in the world of adults. "We know nothing of childhood," wrote Rousseau in his preface, and the accusation is still valid today. In the eyes of his elders, little Émile is a failed version of what they themselves have not become. We adults, then and now, want the young to have the virtues we lack and none of our defects. We educate them to become effective wheels in our machinery, we train them into subservience. We look to what we want and not to what they need. We incite their greed, not their ambition, their cunning, not their intelligence. "Everything is good when it leaves the hands of the Creator; everything degenerates in the hands of man," reads the first line of Rousseau's book. "He maims his dog, his horse, his slave. He topples everything, he disfigures everything; he loves deformity, he loves ghouls. He doesn't want anything as nature made it, not even human beings."

Our Émile today lives in a rundown allotment, in a neglected suburb. For Émile, his neighborhood is a place without mirrors. His identity papers say that he was born somewhere, but according to official statistics he is an undocumented or presumed undocumented person—which, of course, means he came from a non-European country, and not from the United States or Canada. Since Rousseau was fond of botanical metaphors, let us say that our Émile is a kind of weed with unpleasantly visible roots.

Other than those roots, in society's eye, Émile himself has no recognizable identity. In the public imagination, he and his friends are not individuals, only examples of social problems. They are an echo of their undesirable parents and grandparents—also suspicious characters, but ones who at least had the decency to keep quiet, do as they were told, and then die.

To begin his education, to develop his "good nature," the new Émile must first discover what his nature is. He must find a sounding board, but, alas, what is offered to him in the way of common cultural vocabulary is limited. Commercial iconography (of things which he knows he cannot have without money) depicts the world as a material paradise of fast cars and women in frilly underwear, as in the rap videos he watches. Rather than through rational instruction, Émile's everyday schooling is effected by means of ads and electronic games that tell him that happiness can be bought, violence carries no consequence, and the ancient patriarchal norms are still very much in effect. Even knowing that this paradise is for him to a great extent unattainable, Émile sees himself irresistibly attracted to these feverish images, since there is hope in absence.

These temptations are not Émile's only sensual stimuli. Because Émile lives in a democracy, the paradisiacal iconography is accompanied by society's formal offerings, local monuments to its official institutions, at whose altars Émile is expected to worship. Somewhere lost among the high, graceless, battered towers in which he and his friends spend their days are nurseries, schools, recreation centers, churches and mosques, first-aid clinics, employment offices. But these institutions are not felt by Émile as his: they have been built for him, he believes, much as kennels are built for dogs, to be cared for according to what his betters think he deserves and for which he is expected to be mutely grateful. (In this vein, Barbara Bush explained after the New Orleans catastrophe that the survivors should be grateful for having been given something better than what they had had before Hurricane Katrina.) Therefore, to signal his presence, to be immortalized by the media bards of today, to have his face plastered on the television screen, Émile will set these temples on fire. In these acts of desecration there is as much anger as rejoicing. He is called scum? He will behave as scum.

In the third step of his pedagogical path, Rousseau

shows Émile how to work and, pragmatically, the rudiments of a craft. Today, in Émile's world, a job, a good job, is not the common lot. And there are other ways of obtaining the tempting goods. In a world which denies his existence as an individual, crime is an obvious option: not the labyrinthine and colossal crimes of international finance but ordinary, everyday pilfering, pimping, and drug dealing. More or less consciously, Émile believes, with Jean Genet, that breaking the law (which, in any case, does not properly defend his rights) is a way of remaining decent in a corrupt society. "There are two classes of people: those who rob others and those who are robbed" is the word on the street. Émile chooses to belong to the first category, while his parents, he believed, were condemned to the second.

Learning how to earn a living is followed by learning how to behave among one's fellow citizens. In his neighborhood, Émile learns that from the start, especially if he is black, he will be treated by the authorities as a suspect: the choice of the crime is left up to him. Since Émile is branded an outlaw, he must find a secure ground from which to address the self-proclaimed enemy. One of the possibilities offered is the well-publicized paradise of extremism or, more reasonably, a faith he only nebulously understands. In spite of the government's attempts at conciliation, for Émile and his friends the extremist factions of the Islamic State stand as opposition to the arrogant culture that excludes them. Extremism offers them the possibility of rebellion, a strategy of protest, a way of differentiating themselves from those who ignore them.

Finally, Émile becomes an adult. He finds his Sophie,

and they have new Émiles. Will anything change for them? Not really. Caught in a machinery that wants to produce consumers, not citizens, and eking out an existence in the shadow of the same old, corrupt men and women who govern them, the only chance for the future Émiles is to become visible not as cameos on the news but as protagonists of change, as men capable of achieving happiness, which means (to quote Rousseau once again) to "stand up for oneself," since "to be oneself without contradiction is no doubt the true state of happiness."

Rousseau concludes: "The way things are now, someone abandoned from birth to his own devices will become the most rejected of all. Prejudices, authorities, needs, exemplary figures, all the social institutions in which we are plunged will stifle his nature and will not fix anything."

SINBAD

On November 4, 2003, fourteen Kurdish refugees and four Indonesian sailors landed a small ship on the coast of Melville Island, fifty miles north of Darwin, in the territorial waters of Australia, with the intention of demanding political asylum. Apprised of the news, and weary of the tide of asylum seekers, the then prime minister of Australia, John Howard, took a drastic decision: he decided to cut off Melville Island from the nation's territory. The gesture was not novel. In 2001, the Australian government

had already excluded Christmas Island from its borders so as to be able to deport to the island's inhospitable beaches several hundreds of illegal immigrants.

Sometime in the fifth century B.C.E., Plato, citizen of Athens, in order to describe the qualities of his ideal republic, invented an island called Atlantis on which he built an imaginary city that supposedly flourished in the distant past and then was swallowed by the sea. Plato's Atlantis inaugurates a wonderful imaginary geography that has never ceased to grow and that has given us some the most famous, albeit inexistent, places in the world: Utopia, Oz, Shangri-La, the nebulous plot of land that houses the wizarding school of Hogwarts. Because the world we inhabit feels at times too crowded for the purposes of our imagination, we have continuously created other places that, save for the trivial fact of not occupying real space, have brilliantly served as stage for both our nightmares and our lofty aspirations.

For Plato, the invention of an island on which he could construct an imaginary society allowed him to mirror back to his own its merits and its faults. That is why, since the days of the first campfires, we tell stories, and that is why we imagine realms where these stories can take place. Unlike politicians, storytellers know that we cannot sever intellectual reality from material reality: all we are entitled to do is to re-imagine the world in order better to see and understand it. The adventures of Sinbad the Sailor, as told in the *Arabian Nights,* are a way of re-imagining the world by reshuffling the notions of land (where his stories are told) and sea (where they are enacted).

From the moment we say "sea" we are forced to think "land." Sinbad the Sailor is he who is no longer on land, he who flees the coast, he who seeks in that other constantly changing plain a cartography that his blood feels nostalgic for. On firm ground, Sinbad's life is peaceful, repetitive, predictable. Out at sea it is the opposite. In this realm without ballasts, where everything is horizon, anything, even the unimaginable, can and does take place. As Sinbad knows, we all require the challenge of the unknown in order to learn to be prepared for death, that essentially unknown territory. And so, as he lives out with increasing intensity his seafaring adventures, Sinbad is training for the final moment when he will become again dust and return forever to the land. We, readers of his adventures, intuit that this last page is fast approaching because when we flip back to the beginning of the wondrous 537th Arabian Night (in which the Old Sinbad, wealthy and settled in his ways, is about to tell the story of his life), we realize that this peaceful homey image is a foreshadowing of the necessary and nearby end.

We forget that there is not one Sinbad but two. The hero we all know is an explorer of the seas, whose features are those of Douglas Fairbanks and whose voice is Errol Flynn's or Brad Pitt's, but there is another Sinbad, the earthbound Sinbad, a certain Sinbad the Carrier, whom Sinbad the Sailor invites back to his house, according to Scheherazade's telling over almost thirty nights. For Sinbad the Sailor to exist, Sinbad the Carrier must also be present, and it is only when the two are face to face that the story within the story can unfold.

The seven adventures of Sinbad the Sailor are hair-raising. The young hero is plunged into the depths of the sea when the island he has landed on turns out to be a whale (an experience shared with the good Saint Brendan of Ireland). He is carried off into the clouds by a giant bird that calls itself a Roc. He battles, like his forerunner Odysseus, with hordes of cannibalistic one-eyed giants, and also with poisonous snakes. He faces, like Tripitak, hideous ghosts who want to drink his blood. He is captured by the Old Man of the Sea and is forced to carry the aged fiend on his shoulders. He is pursued by pirates whose ultimate destiny, like his own, is a watery grave. But we would not know of these adventures were it not for the other for whom these tales are told, the listener, Sinbad the Earthbound.

In this way, Sinbad's sea of stories becomes never-ending. Sinbad the Sailor tells his story to Sinbad the Carrier; what Sinbad the Carrier hears is voiced by the clever Scheherazade. Scheherazade's telling is apparently intended for the ears of her sister Dunyazade, but what Dunyazade hears is also and above all heard by the vengeful King Shahryar. Shahryar's eavesdropping becomes the tale we ourselves witness, our ear against the keyhole of a door that leads to a long corridor of ancient echoes.

WAKEFIELD

When I was five or six years old, I had a recurring
daydream. I imagined that I was kidnapped by a gang of
land pirates (for some reason, they lacked a ship and went
about on foot) and taken far away to a mountainous place
somewhat like Heidi's grandfather's home, where I was
taught all sorts of fascinating things. I suppose we all, at
some point or another, imagine a life very different from
the one we lead, and without our turning into Walter
Mittys the life not led becomes in many ways more vivid

and important than the one we follow daily. The Platonic myth of the original split self condemned to seek the lost half is, I believe, a fairly common experience: we long for the experience of the self we cannot be.

According to a certain Dr. William King, in his *Anecdotes of His Own Times* published in 1818, a gentleman named Howe one day left his wife without a word of explanation and only returned to her after a period of many years. Nathaniel Hawthorne came across this snippet, told by King as true, and rewrote it under the name he gave to the odd adventurer, "Wakefield." Wakefield, Hawthorne tells us, under pretense of going on a journey takes lodgings in the street next to his own, and there, without communicating with his wife or friends, and "without the shadow of a reason for such self-banishment," lives in quiet isolation for over twenty years. After a time, certain that her husband has met with a fatal accident, Mrs. Wakefield resigns herself to an "autumnal widowhood." Then one evening, as if returning from a single day's absence, Wakefield enters his house again and, Hawthorne concludes, becomes "a loving spouse till death."

Hawthorne attempts to imagine who Wakefield was before he walked out of his ordinary life without knowing what would happen to him after he made the decision that, at the time, did not seem momentous. Middle-aged, of nonviolent matrimonial affections "sobered into a calm habitual sentiment," Wakefield is the most constant of husbands "because a certain sluggishness would keep his heart at rest, wherever it might be placed." His mind occupied itself in long and lazy musings that tended to no purpose. Had his friends been asked who was the man in

London surest to perform nothing today which should be remembered tomorrow, they would have thought of Wakefield. Only his wife, perhaps, might have hesitated because she might have been aware of a little indefinable strangeness in her husband, a peculiar sort of vanity, a disposition to keep petty secrets hardly worth revealing, a quiet selfishness. "Selfishness," wrote Hawthorne in one of his *Notebooks,* "is one of the qualities most apt to inspire love."

Reflecting on Wakefield's mysterious decision, Hawthorne wonders whether "an influence, beyond our control" does not lay its strong hand on every deed we do, and "weaves its consequences into an iron tissue of necessity." Even when, after ten years' separation, he meets by chance his wife on the street in the midst of a crowd, Wakefield finds himself incapable of stepping back into his relinquished life. In that instant, Mrs. Wakefield may have had the impression of recognizing something or someone, but she passes on, while Wakefield feels that although "all the miserable strangeness of his life" is revealed to him suddenly, he can only cry out: "Wakefield! Wakefield! You are mad!" Perhaps he is, but that explanation does not satisfy us.

Madness may underlie Wakefield's behavior but the explanation does not address the question of its consequences. Once we take the unexpected turn, once we choose the unforeseen path that steers us away from the predetermined goal, what changes in us and in our surroundings? How does another turn of the screw (to use Henry James's image) affect the ways of the world? Even if we could follow two branches of the road at the same time, would anything be different for us? It is told that after the death of Eurydice, Orpheus asked the gods in Hades for the impossible: to allow his beloved to come back to life. The gods granted his request on one condition: Orpheus was forbidden to turn his head to see her. But here is the fatal conundrum: As long as she remains unseen, Eurydice is there, and Orpheus has his wish. But as soon as he turns to look at her, she melts away, and for this he is to blame. So either way, there is nothing there for Orpheus to see, and Orpheus loses his gamble and becomes an outcast.

Hawthorne concludes his story with these words: "Amid the seeming confusion of our mysterious world, individuals are so nicely adjusted to a system, and systems to one another, and to a whole, that, by stepping aside for a moment, a man exposes himself to a fearful risk of losing his place for ever. Like Wakefield, he may become, as it were, the Outcast of the Universe."

Borges noted that Wakefield, like the tragic heroes of Kafka, is distinguished by "a profound triviality which contrasts with the magnitude of his perdition and delivers him, even more helpless, to the Furies." Wakefield's attempt to crack, however slightly, the adamantine course of things is not unique. Gulliver, in the chronicle of his adventures on the Flying Island of Laputa, tells of a great court lady who suddenly decides to leave her quiet life on the island and escapes to the Kingdom of Lagado, where she hides herself for several months, until the King sends a warrant ordering a search for her, and she is found "in an obscure eating-house all in rags, having pawned her clothes to maintain an old deformed footman, who beat her every day." E. L. Doctorow, in a short story also titled "Wakefield," and Eduardo Berti, in his novel *Mrs. Wakefield,* attempted to explore the consequences of such rebellious trivialities. The conclusions are disheartening.

Rumi, the greatest of Sufi mystics, tells this fable (taken up later by Somerset Maugham, Jean Cocteau, and Frank O'Hara): A young man goes to the Prophet Suleiman and says to him: "I was in your city, and Azrael, the Angel of Death, came and stared at me. I beg that you send me off to another country because I don't want to die." On hearing this, Suleiman agreed and commanded the wind to take the man all the way to India. That afternoon, Suleiman summoned Azrael and asked him: "Why did you scare one of my men by staring at him, so that he asked me to send him away all the way to India?" Azrael replied: "O Prophet, the reason why I stared at him like that was because God had commanded me to take this young man tomorrow in India, and I was surprised to see him today walking in the streets of this city."

The choice of the life not lived and the path not taken is tempting because we imagine that had we but done this or undertaken that, things would be different, and we would be happier, wiser, better loved, better respected.

Perhaps not.

SOURCES

Translations of quotations in the text are mine unless another translator is listed.

Monsieur Bovary: Gustave Flaubert, *Madame Bovary*
Little Red Riding Hood: "Little Red Riding Hood," *Grimms' Fairy Tales,* trans. Margaret Hunt, rev. James Stern (London: Routledge and Kegan Paul, 1975)
Dracula: Bram Stoker, *Dracula*
Alice: Lewis Carroll, *Alice's Adventures in Wonderland* and *Through the Looking-Glass and What Alice Found There*
Faust: Christopher Marlowe, *The Tragical History of the Life and Death of Doctor Faustus;* Johann Wolfgang von Goethe, *Faust,* trans. Walter Kaufman (New York: Anchor Books, 1961/1990), and the original German edition
Gertrude: William Shakespeare, *Hamlet*
Superman: Jerry Siegel and Joe Shuster, *Superman* (Marvel comics); George Bernard Shaw, *Man and Superman;* G. K. Chesterton, "How I Found the Superman," in *Alarms and Discursions;* Friedrich Nietzsche, *Thus Spake Zarathustra,* in *A Nietzsche Reader,* trans. R. J. Hollingdale (London: Penguin, 2017)
Don Juan: Molière, *Dom Juan, ou Le Festin de pierre* (Don Juan; or, The Stone Guest); Wolfgang Amadeus Mozart and Lorenzo Da Ponte, *Il dissoluto punito, ossia il Don Giovanni* (The Rake Punished, Namely Don Giovanni); Tirso de Molina, *El*

burlador de Sevilla o el convidado de piedra (The Trickster of Seville and the Stone Guest); George Gordon, Lord Byron, *Don Juan;* José Zorrilla, *Don Juan Tenorio*

Lilith: *The Book of Legends: Sefer Ha-Aggadah; Legends from the Talmud and Midrash,* ed. Hayyim Nahman Bialik and Yehoshua Hana Ravnitzky, trans. William G. Braude (New York: Schocken, 1992); *The Talmud: A Selection,* trans. and ed. Norman Solomon (London: Penguin, 2009)

The Wandering Jew: *Kurze Beschreibung und Erzählung von einem Juden mit Namen Ahasverus* (Short Description and Account of a Jew Named Ahasverus, 1602); Eugène Sue, *Le Juif errant* (The Wandering Jew); Carlo Fruttero and Franco Lucentini, *L'amante senza fissa dimora* (The Lover of No Fixed Abode); Jorge Luis Borges, "El Inmortal" (The Immortal) in *El Aleph* (The Aleph)

Sleeping Beauty: "La Belle au bois dormant" (Sleeping Beauty in the Woods), Charles Perrault, *Contes* (Fairy Tales); "Little Briar Rose," *Grimms' Fairy Tales,* trans. Margaret Hunt, rev. James Stern (London: Routledge and Kegan Paul, 1975)

Phoebe: J. D. Salinger, *The Catcher in the Rye*

Hsing-chen: Kim Man-jung, *The Nine Cloud Dream,* trans. Heinz Insu Fenkl (New York: Penguin, 2019)

Jim: Mark Twain, *Adventures of Huckleberry Finn*

The Chimera: Homer, *The Iliad,* trans. Richmond Lattimore (Chicago: University of Chicago Press, 1951); Hesiod, *Theogony,* trans. Dorothea Wender (Harmondsworth, UK: Penguin, 1986); Robert Graves, *The Greek Myths* (London: Penguin, 1993)

Robinson Crusoe: Daniel Defoe, *The Life and Strange Surprizing Adventures of Robinson Crusoe, of York, Mariner*

Queequeg: Herman Melville, *Moby-Dick; or, The Whale*

Tyrant Banderas: Ramón del Valle-Inclán, *Tyrant Banderas,* trans. Edith Grossman (New York: NYRB Classics, 2012)

Cide Hamete Benegeli: Miguel de Cervantes, *Don Quixote*

Job: Job (Bible); Moses Maimonides, *Guide of the Perplexed,* 2 vols., trans. Shlomo Pines (Chicago: University of Chicago Press, 1963)

Quasimodo: Victor Hugo, *Notre-Dame de Paris* (The Hunchback of Notre-Dame)

Casaubon: George Eliot, *Middlemarch: A Study of Provincial Life*

Satan: Jubilees (Apocrypha); Dante, *La commedia* (The Divine Comedy); John Milton, *Paradise Lost;* Peter J. Awn, *Satan's Tragedy and Redemption: Iblīs in Sufi Psychology* (Leiden: Brill, 1983) (for Al-Ghazali); Stephen Greenblatt, *The Rise and Fall of Adam and Eve: The Story That Created Us* (New York: Norton, 2018) (for Shihab al-Din al-Nuwayri and late Qur'anic exegetes); Johann Wolfgang von Goethe, *Faust,* trans. Walter Kaufman (New York: Anchor Books, 1961/1990), and the original German edition

The Hippogriff: Ludovico Ariosto, *Orlando Furioso* (The Frenzy of Orlando)

Captain Nemo: Jules Verne, *Twenty Thousand Leagues Under the Sea* (translation adapted from Lewis Page Mercier) and *The Mysterious Island*

Frankenstein's Monster: Mary Shelley, *Frankenstein; or, The Modern Prometheus; Frankenstein* (Universal Studios, 1931)

Sandy: Wu Ch'êng-ên [Cheng'en], *Monkey: Folk Novel of China,* trans. Arthur Waley (New York: Grove, 1970)

Jonah: Jonah (Bible)

Dona Emilia: José Bento Renato Monteiro Lobato, *A Menina do Narizinho Arrebitado* (The Girl with the Turned-Up Nose), *O Picapau Amarelo* (The Yellow Woodpecker Ranch), and *Serões de Dona Benta* (Night Chatting with Mrs. Benta)

The Wendigo: John Robert Colombo, ed., *Windigo: An*

Anthology of Fact and Fantastic Fiction (Lincoln: University of Nebraska Press, 1983)

Heidi's Grandfather: Johanna Spyri, *Heidi*

Clever Elsie: "Clever Elsie," *Grimms' Fairy Tales,* trans. Margaret Hunt, rev. James Stern (London: Routledge and Kegan Paul, 1975)

Long John Silver: Robert Louis Stevenson, *Treasure Island*

Karagöz and Hacivat: *Selected Stories of Hacivat and Karagöz,* ed. Zeynep Üstün, trans. Havva Aslan (Istanbul: Profil, 2008)

Émile: Jean-Jacques Rousseau, *Émile, ou De l'éducation* (Émile; or, On Education)

Sinbad: *Les Mille et une nuits: Contes arabes* (an 1823 French translation; in English *The Thousand and One Nights* or *The Arabian Nights*)

Wakefield: Nathaniel Hawthorne, "Wakefield," *Twice-Told Tales*

Additional quotations not identified in the text are taken from the following; translations are mine unless otherwise identified.

Alcott, Louisa May, *Little Women*

Aquinas, Thomas, *Summa Theologica,* trans. Fathers of the English Dominican Province (New York: Benziger Brothers, 1947)

Aristotle, *Politics,* trans. Benjamin Jowett

Augustine, *The City of God,* trans. Marcus Dods, 3 vols. (Edinburgh: T. & T. Clark, 1888), vol. 2

Blumenberg, Hans, *Shipwreck with Spectator: Paradigm of a Metaphor for Existence,* trans. Steven Rendall (Cambridge: MIT Press, 1996)

Borges, Jorge Luis, "Alexander Selkirk," in *El otro, el mismo* (The Other, the Same), trans. Stephen Kessler, in Jorge Luis

Borges, *Selected Poems,* ed. Alexander Coleman (New York: Viking Books; London: Allen Lane/Penguin Press, 1999).

Browne, Thomas, *Religio Medici*

Calderón de la Barca, Pedro, *La vida es sueño* (Life Is a Dream)

Choisy, abbot of (François Timoléon), *Mémoires* (Memoirs)

Douglass, Frederick, *The Life and Times of Frederick Douglass*

Die Edda (Prose Edda), "Das Thrymlied" (The Lay of Thrym), in *Die Isländersagas,* ed. Klaus Böld, Andreas Vollmer and Julia Zernack, 4 vols. (Frankfurt-am-Main: Fischer Verlag, 2011)

Eisenstein, Elizabeth L., *The Printing Press as an Agent of Change* (Cambridge: Cambridge University Press, 1980)

Euripides, *Fragments,* vol. 7: *Aegeus–Meleager,* ed. and trans. Christopher Collard and Martin Cropp (Cambridge: Harvard University Press, 2008)

Goethe, Johann Wolfgang von, *West-östlicher Divan* (West-East Divan)

Hedayat, Sadegh, *The Blind Owl and Other Hedayat Stories,* ed. Russell P. Christensen, trans. Iraj Bashiri (Minneapolis: Sorayya, 1985)

Homer, *The Odyssey,* trans. Samuel Butler (London: A. C. Fifield, 1900) (translation modified, including changing "Ulysses" to "Odysseus")

Jung, Carl Gustav, "Commentary on 'The Secret of the Golden Flower,'" in *Alchemical Studies,* trans. R. F. C. Hull (Princeton: Princeton University Press, 1957).

Laux, Dorianne, "Superman," *The Book of Men: Poems* (New York: Norton, 2011)

Luis de Góngora y Argote, "Soneto" (sometimes titled "A un sueño" or "Varia imaginación . . ."), in *Sonetos completos*

Magritte, René, "Ligne de vie" (Lifeline), in *Écrits complets* (Complete Writings) (Paris: Flammarion, 1979)

Malraux, André, *La voie royale* (The Way of Kings)

Miles, Jack, *God: A Biography* (New York: Random House, 1995)

Neruda, Pablo, *Veinte poemas de amor y una canción desesperada* (Twenty Love Poems and a Song of Despair), poem 15

Nietzsche, Friedrich, *Ecce Homo: Wie man wird, was man ist* (Ecce Homo: How One Becomes What One Is)

Plato, *Republic,* trans. Paul Shorey, in *The Collected Dialogues,* ed. Edith Hamilton and Huntington Cairns (Princeton: Princeton University Press, 1961)

Proudhon, Pierre-Joseph, *Solution du problème social* (Solution to the Social Problem)

Proust, Marcel, *La prisonnière* (The Captive)

Rulfo, Juan, "¿No oyes ladrar los perros?" (Can't You Hear the Dogs Bark?), in *El Llano en llamas*

Sade, marquis de, *Justine; ou, Les malheurs de la vertu* (Justine; or, The Misfortunes of Virtue)

Sartwell, Crispin, *Six Names of Beauty* (London: Routledge, 2004)

Scève, Maurice, "La gorge" (The Neck), in *Délie, objet de plus haute vertu* (Délie: Object of Highest Virtue)

Scott, Walter, *Rokeby: A Poem*

Shakespeare, William, *Romeo and Juliet; King Lear*

Stevenson, Robert Louis, "El Dorado," in *Virginibus Puerisque*

Tolstoy, Lev, *The Death of Ivan Ilyich and Other Stories,* trans. Louise and Aylmer Maude (Jerusalem: Minerva Publishing, 2018)

Veyne, Paul, *Did the Greeks Believe in Their Myths? An Essay on the Constitutive Imagination,* trans. Paula Wissing (Chicago: University of Chicago Press, 1988)

ACKNOWLEDGMENTS

Thanks to my editor and reader, John Donatich, for his acute insights and enthusiastic encouragement.

Thanks to Danielle D'Orlando, Acquisitions Department Manager, for her patience and help.

Thanks to the designer, Nancy Ovedovitz, for her brilliant imagination and care.

As always, thanks to my agents, Guillermo Schavelzon and Barbara Graham, for their persistent confidence.

Special thanks to Susan Laity, Senior Manuscript Editor, for having done her utmost to keep Titivillus, imp of typos and factual errors, at bay. Titivillus (Susan will no doubt check this) first appeared in the *Tractatus de penitentia* by the late-thirteenth-century Franciscan scholar Johannes Walensis (John of Wales), who blamed the imp for the many mistakes that occurred in his scriptorium.

Infinite thanks to Jillian Tomm, dear friend and passionate reader, who inspected these monsters as they kept appearing one by one, and got them to polish their nails, comb their hair, and tuck in their tattered shirts.

And to Craig, as always, with all my love.

A few of these monsters, in different versions, appeared earlier in Spanish, first in a limited edition of Del Centro Editores in Madrid with illustrations by Antonio Seguí, and then published by Alianza Editorial, S.A., also with the Seguí illustrations.

CREDITS